AF599174

THE CROOKED PLACES MADE STRAIGHT

ALSO BY RAPHAEL G. WARNOCK

The Divided Mind of the Black Church: Theology, Piety, and Public Witness

A Way Out of No Way: A Memoir of Truth, Transformation, and the New American Story

Put Your Shoes On & Get Ready!

We're in This Together: Leo's Lunch Box

THE CROOKED PLACES MADE STRAIGHT

Reflections on the Moral Meaning of America

Raphael G. Warnock

PENGUIN PRESS
NEW YORK
2026

PENGUIN PRESS
An imprint of Penguin Random House LLC
1745 Broadway, New York, NY 10019
penguinrandomhouse.com

DESIGNED BY MEIGHAN CAVANAUGH

LIBRARY OF CONGRESS CATALOGING-IN-PUBLICATION DATA

Names: Warnock, Raphael G. author
Title: The crooked places made straight : reflections on the moral meaning of America / Raphael G. Warnock.
Description: New York : Penguin Press, 2026. | Includes bibliographical references and index.
Identifiers: LCCN 2025043956 (print) | LCCN 2025043957 (ebook) | ISBN 9798217058983 hardcover | ISBN 9798217058990 ebook
Subjects: LCSH: United States—Politics and government—2021– | United States—Social conditions—2020– | Social values—United States | Political rights—United States | Political rights—Religious aspects—Christianity | Bible. Isaiah
Classification: LCC E894 .W37 2026 (print) | LCC E894 (ebook) | DDC 320.473092—dc23/eng/20260223
LC record available at https://lccn.loc.gov/2025043956
LC ebook record available at https://lccn.loc.gov/2025043957

Printed in the United States of America
2nd Printing

The authorized representative in the EU for product safety and compliance is Penguin Random House Ireland, Morrison Chambers, 32 Nassau Street, Dublin D02 YH68, Ireland, https://eu-contact.penguin.ie.

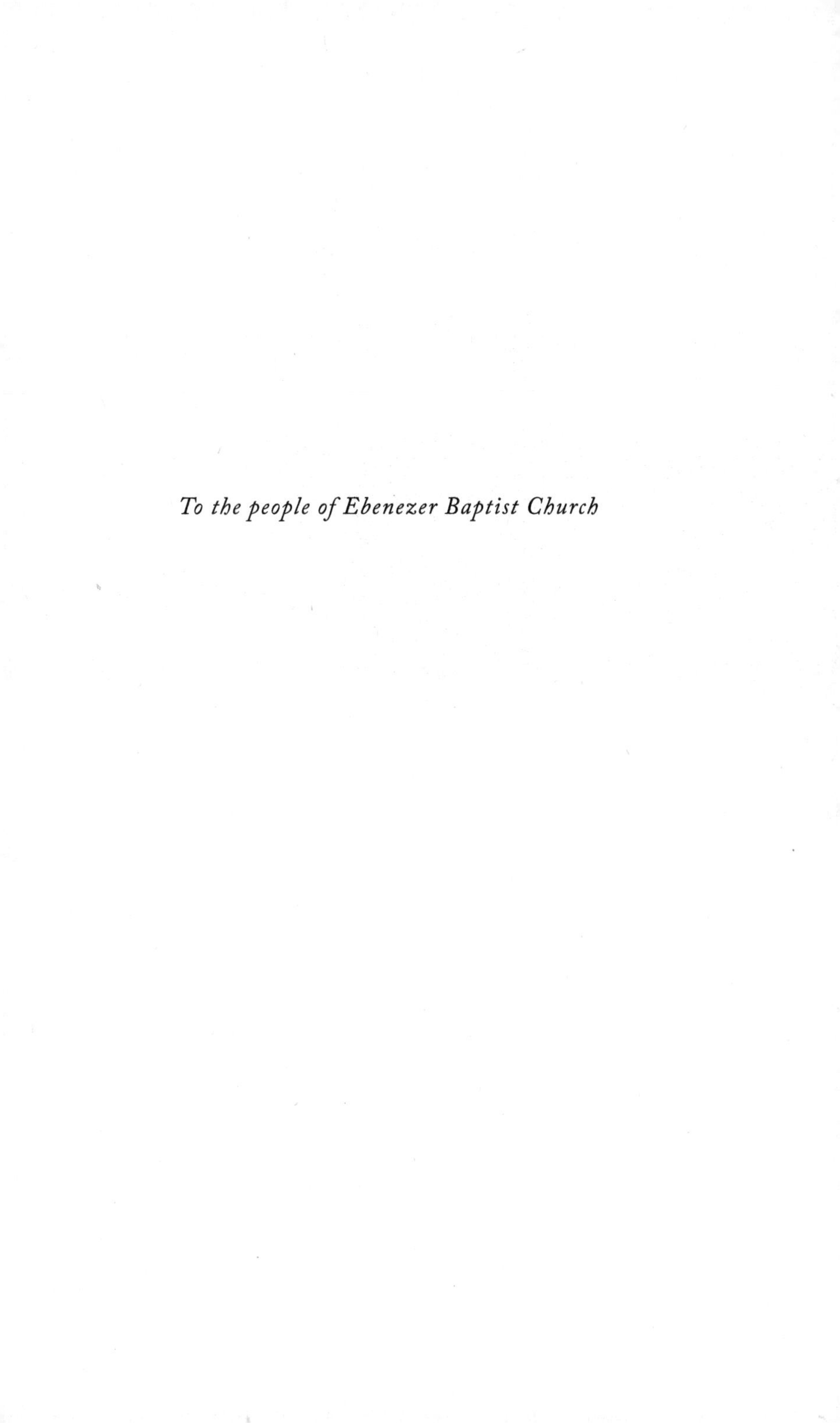

To the people of Ebenezer Baptist Church

CONTENTS

INTRODUCTION

AMERICA, THE GRAND CATHEDRAL

Even before I began preaching one Sunday morning in June 2023, I thought about the miracle of that moment. I was about to deliver a sermon recognizing Juneteenth as a federal holiday from the pulpit of Washington National Cathedral. U.S. presidents had addressed the nation from where I stood. Others had been mourned by dignitaries from across the globe in this sacred space. A decade earlier, I had stood there delivering the closing prayer for the ecumenical service at President Barack Obama's second inauguration.

And there I was again. A black boy raised in public housing who, in the years since Obama's inauguration as the first black president, had become the first black United States senator from Georgia. A Baptist preacher, invited to address a cathedral full of folks from all kinds of religious and ethnic backgrounds. A longtime activist, standing before a multiracial congregation in the nation's capital to acknowledge Emancipation Day, the end of slavery, as our shared history.

Mindful of the diverse crowd abiding together for the occasion, I offered a bit of levity and a callout to my church, Ebenezer Baptist in Atlanta, spiritual home to Dr. Martin Luther King Jr. Dr. King preached his final Sunday sermon from the pulpit of the National Cathedral just four days before his death. It was titled "Remaining Awake Through a Great Revolution." "I'm going to get on with the sermon," I began that morning. "But I'm going to ask you to meet me halfway, because in my church they talk back to me."

A few members of the congregation straightened their backs, sitting taller.

I explained the traditional black church's call-and-response, where talking back to the preacher sends a strong message of support. Among Episcopalians, who fill this sanctuary most Sunday mornings, talking while the pastor is talking might seem rude—a difference we Baptists highlight lovingly when we refer to them as "the frozen chosen." So I invited the audience members to practice.

"If I say something that you agree with, just say 'Amen,'" I said.

They politely followed suit.

"If I say something that you agree with, but it's a tough saying, it's hard, it challenges us, say 'Have mercy!'"

Actually, in the impassioned colloquialisms of the black Baptist tradition, I told them, the two words are often collapsed into one. Say "Hammercy!" The congregants laughed softly while saying "Hammercy!"

"Now, if I say something that you don't agree with at all, but you know we're all in here together, trying to get through this together, say 'Lord, help!'"

They laughed louder.

They got what I was really saying: that despite our differences, we would be all right, communing with one another and with God for a short while in this grand cathedral. In fact, this diverse gathering of humanity affirming our faith and imagining a future big enough to embrace all of us was a small glimpse of God's dream for the world! That work is and always will be a group project.

In that sense, the massive architecture of our shared future is akin to the very place where we were gathered. Washington National Cathedral is the sixth-largest Gothic cathedral in the world and took eighty-three years to complete. Cathedrals take a long time to build because their structures are vast, intricate, complicated, and ornate. They are also costly and thus are sometimes delayed by the fluctuations of the economy, political instability, or even wars. Skilled artisans and builders sign up for the honor of contributing to such a masterpiece, but even as they work, they recognize that they likely will not live to see the completion of the majestic marvel that they are helping to construct. Yet the role that each of them plays is crucial to shaping the full magnificence to come.

Construction of the Cathedral of St. John the Divine in New York City began in 1892, and although it was consecrated and opened to the public in 1941, only two-thirds of the original plan is complete. That is why it is nicknamed "St. John the Unfinished." Standing in the grand pulpit of the National Cathedral that morning, I reflected that America is like a glorious cathedral, 250 years in the making. Yet, after all these years, we're still wrestling and toiling to build this grand cathedral of freedom and democracy. Words from the poet Langston Hughes come to mind: "America never was America to me, / And yet I swear this oath— / America will be!"

For my message on that glorious Juneteenth weekend, I found inspiration in the ancient wisdom of the biblical prophet Isaiah, whose words I have been preaching in sermons across the length and breadth of our nation for many years. In the book of Isaiah, chapter 40, God speaks a word of hope to a people physically and politically exiled, a people spiritually and emotionally exhausted. It's such a tough time that God tells the prophet, "Comfort my people" and "speak tenderly" to them.

Isaiah responds to the call with a kind of moral topography. A justice-centered geography. God's great vision for the land. The words are familiar to Jews and Christians alike, and to anyone who has ever heard the spectacular sounds of George Frideric Handel's *Messiah*. Isaiah imagines a future with hope:

> Every valley shall be exalted, and every mountain and hill brought low; The crooked places shall be made straight, and the rough places smooth; And the glory of the Lord shall be revealed, and all flesh shall see it together. (ISAIAH 40:4–5, NKJV)

The ethical import of this ancient text and its continuing relevance for our times captured the imagination of the preacher. I told the congregation that in God's vision for the land, first of all valleys are exalted, and mountains and hills are made low. We live in a time when increasingly the high sit very high and the low sit very low. Vast wealth inequality seems intractable, and it is getting worse, with tragic implications not only for the poor and working class but for the future of the whole land! But in God's vision for the land, there is equity. The low places are enabled to come up a little higher, and the high places come down a little lower. It is a message of hope at the end of a long, dark night. After a period of deep suffering and exile, the prophet speaks not merely of a return *to* the land but a bold reimagining *of* the land. As we return once again to the meaning of America, on the occasion of the nation's 250th anniversary of its independence, I ask, what might it mean to imagine a future where valleys are exalted and mountains and hills are made low?

Indeed, Isaiah's words are so beautiful, so sublime, that they cut right through the hopelessness of a people awash in despair. How we need this kind of bold vision in a moment like our own! The truth is that the partisan and petty rhetoric of politics today is simply too puny a language for the magnitude of the problems we face. Instead, I urge us to look to Isaiah as a lens through which to view the problems that confront us and the possibilities within and around us. The goal of this book is to lay out that vision clearly so that we can work together to build the America that we want to see.

In sharp contrast to the narrow, individualistic obsession that characterizes so much of American preaching, the eighth-century prophets of the Bible addressed their preachments to the social order. In God's vision, as expressed through Isaiah, not only is there equity, but there is *integrity*, *possibility*, and *inclusivity*. There is a shared commitment to a social vision that honors the humanity of all. I offer "the crooked places . . . made straight" as a way of talking about the integrity so badly needed in our politics and nation today. "The rough places smooth" reminds us that there is also possibility. The prophet is saying: I know it's dark right now, but the light shines through the darkness, transforming dismal conditions and making rough places smooth. The last part, "and all flesh shall see it together," is about inclusivity, the inextricable connection we have with one another.

Isaiah is helpful in our context because his poetic language calls upon us to anchor ourselves in the best of our moral traditions and reimagine the future. In that sense, his moral topography is a bold, countervailing vision about how to live and relate to one another in the land and how we relate to the land itself. It is a geopolitics that reverences creation and centers love and justice. No wonder Isaiah's words have been remixed by every Gospel writer of the Christian New Testament and sampled across the centuries! In the way of prophets and poets, he helps us to see ourselves through a moral prism and, with his feet firmly on the ground, he imagines new possibilities.

I used to read this text and think that what it meant was that the glory of God is so grand, so overwhelming, so extraordinary, that when God's glory is revealed, all flesh cannot help but to see it. Nowadays, I read it in the reverse. In fact, I think the prophet is teaching us *how* to see the glory of God. In order to see God, we must first behold one another in our rich and variegated human beauty. In the eyes of the other, we get a glimpse of the glory of God. "All flesh shall see it together."

Yet there is despair and doubt that it will ever come. Isaiah sees it, and I feel it. He asks, "How long, O Lord?" A question I, too, find myself asking, over and over again. Our country needs moral leadership and a renewed vision like Isaiah's, one that invites us to reach out to one another, to pray for one another rather than prey on one another, and to reach toward our highest and noblest ideals rather than sink in our basest fears. To turn to what Abraham Lincoln called at another time of deep division "the better angels of our nature." I so deeply believe in Isaiah's vision for a reimagined moral topography that I use his principles and teachings as my guidepost. They provide for me a gut check for my public work. I commend them for our collective consideration.

Isaiah's prophetic utterances come against the backdrop of one of the lowest points in ancient Israel's history—a time that is a far cry from the height of the nation's power. In fact, the nation has been weakened. The people have been ejected from familiar places and signposts that provide certainty and meaning. It was a time much like the America we see today. We have found ourselves living in a strange land.

Although the book of Isaiah bears the name of one individual—whose name literally means "the Lord saves"—

these passages cover a longer period, beyond the span of a single life, to include the reigns of several kings and Israel's subjugation to several succeeding empires. And the book is not written by just one person. Writings by several authors together form what Bible scholars call "the Isaiah tradition."

This tradition addressed a people in exile, cast out to a foreign and unfamiliar land. Theirs is a political crisis with psychic and emotional implications. All the landmarks that gave them a sense of security, including the Temple, are in flux. There is a vacuum in leadership. The future seems uncertain, and the people are desperately insecure, wondering if they will ever find their way back home. But through Isaiah, we see that these moments are also opportunities for new leadership and new possibilities.

Given the prominence of the theme of justice (*mispat*) in the Hebrew prophetic tradition, it is not surprising to see this theme emerge over and again in Isaiah's writings. He provides spiritual and social commentary on his times through the lens of faith. His is not a spooky spirituality, disembodied and disconnected from the real world. Rather, it is rooted in lived experience and the physical world, fully engaged with its geopolitical complexity, ecological perils, and social problems. His words are not easy. In fact, his message is often quite harsh, administering the bitter medicine and tough love that prophets provide. But ultimately, it leans into hope.

Isaiah is no stranger to frustration with institutional leadership. He knows well the perils of public corruption, sophisticated legalized bribery, and a political class more interested in preserving its own power than in serving the people. We feel the turmoil in Isaiah's words as he criticizes his people, who should have known better, and done better. He's fed up with political leaders who are focused on their own gain at the expense of the people. "Your princes are rebels and companions of thieves," he says in Isaiah 1:22–24 (NRSVA). "Everyone loves a bribe and runs after gifts. They do not defend the orphan, and the widow's cause does not come before them," he continues, referring to the most downtrodden, weak, and forgotten members of society. When I consider the overwhelming influence of dark money and big monied interests and corporations in our politics, I think Isaiah might well have been speaking of twenty-first-century American politicians.

Isaiah's voice emerges at a time of tectonic changes, much like our own. We, too, live in a kind of exile; that is, we are increasingly disconnected from one another in a sea of technological hyper-connectivity. This has deeply impacted our children, who too often live in lonely silos curated by the algorithms of big technology companies that have left them depressed, disconnected from authentic, human relationships, and sometimes suicidal. Moreover, all of this is happening within the larger context of an American crisis of cynicism and despair in which the American people are understandably frustrated, and many have lost faith, confidence, and trust in the major institutions of society: the government, police, the Supreme Court, media, banking, and houses of faith.

But Isaiah is not only frustrated with unprincipled political leadership. He also chastises religious leaders and institutions whose outward piety and worship show no mercy to the most marginalized members of the human family. He avers, "I cannot endure solemn assemblies with iniquity. . . . Even though you make many prayers, I will not listen; your hands are full of blood. . . . Seek justice, rescue the oppressed, defend the orphan, plead for the widow." The Hebrew prophetic tradition is a prominent part of Scripture that challenges the excesses and machinations of power among the Israelites. But unlike so many of today's ministers whose messages to the people center on personal piety, the Hebrew prophets focused on systemic injustice. This challenge and call to center the humanity of the weak was central to their work. But you wouldn't know that listening to the loudest and most well-financed Christian voices in our country today. Rather than hating the condition of poverty, as in Isaiah's prophetic tradition, they choose to hate poor people and blame them for their condition. Not only is such a stance unjust, but it is also unwise. Public policy that leaves so many behind can only leave our nation poorer, sicker, and weaker.

Somebody say, "Amen!!!"

Indeed, a survey conducted by the Kaiser Family Foundation and *The Washington Post* after Donald Trump's first election showed that Christians, particularly white Evangelicals, were much more likely than non-Christians to blame poverty on individual failings rather than on difficult circumstances beyond their control. According to the poll, 53 percent of white Evangelicals, more than any other religious group, blamed lack of effort for a person's poverty. The poll also showed that 63 percent of Republicans held this viewpoint, compared with 26 percent of Democrats. White Evangelicals have overwhelmingly supported Trump and used their voices and votes to lift him to the highest office in the land twice. Now, with Republicans controlling both houses of Congress and Trump in his second term, the poorest of the poor and the most marginalized members of the human family are again the least protected and the most vulnerable to his heartless policies and practices.

I can hear the voices, shouting far and wide, "*Hammercy!*"

Over these past months, Trump and his administration have been doing all they can to reshape government based on the vision of the Heritage Foundation's Project 2025, the ultraconservative blueprint that calls for vastly expanding presidential power, shrinking government, and getting rid of some tried-and-true programs that give poor people a boost. That includes the venerable Head Start, which provides poor children early access to education. I know firsthand the value of Head Start, because I attended the program as a poor kid, growing up with two hardworking parents in Savannah, Georgia. Head Start sparked my intellectual curiosity and put me on a path to a prosperous and productive life, as it has done for millions of children over the past six decades. Deep in my spirit, I hear the God of Isaiah ask, "What do you mean by crushing my people and grinding the faces of the poor?" I can hear Jesus saying, "I came to preach good news to the poor." In God's vision for the land, valleys are exalted, mountains and hills are made low. In God's vision, there is equity.

To get more equity in the land, however, we desperately need more integrity. More leaders committed to truth, regardless of party politics. Leaders with their feet firmly planted in a vision of America signified by the Declaration of Independence, the Emancipation Proclamation, and the nation's highest ideals. Leaders like my late mentor and parishioner, U.S. Representative John R. Lewis, who stood for truth and justice, walked out his faith, and put his body on the line to help smooth the rough places at a critical moment in the sculpting of our great land of the free.

We are the latest generation of Americans to find ourselves standing at a critical crossroads in our nation's history. "We the people" have a sense that something is profoundly broken, and we are right. A recent Pew Research Center survey found that most Americans, 63 percent, are very or somewhat pessimistic about the country's "moral and ethical standards." We sense, collectively, that an urgent crossroads is upon us. Beneath the cacophonous noise, chaos, and anger in our politics and public life, there is a gnawing spiritual hunger. Something is missing in our family conversation; there is an unmistakable void in our public discourse. People of various religious traditions feel it. So, too, do those who say they are spiritual but not religious, as well as those who make no such claims at all. Tellingly, this latter group—29 percent of American adults, who say they are "religiously unaffiliated"—had been growing for years, while the percentage of Americans who identify as Christians—40 percent of whom are Protestant and 19 percent Catholic—had been declining.

Honestly, there are days when I find that I must labor assiduously just to beat back the shadows of despair lurking in my own heart. I've spent much of my life fighting for racial justice, and yet I, like so many, have found myself taken aback, especially during Trump's second presidential term, by the sheer intractability of it all. After all he has done to destroy the progress of generations past to make America a more diverse, equitable, and inclusive place. After all he has done to divide us, to make the poor poorer and the rich richer. After all this, so many of my white Evangelical Christian sisters and brothers choose to look the other way, to remain silent, to continue making excuses for the president's anti-Christian behavior.

Trump was boldly transparent about his warped vision for America on the campaign trail. In a speech less than four months before the November 2024 election, then-candidate Trump urged Christians to show up for him at the polls and offered this inimical view of America: "In four years, you don't have to vote again. We'll have it fixed so good, you're not going to have to vote." And from day one of his presidency, he's been trying to make good on that promise, behaving like the dictator he'd pledged to become.

Just hours after Trump's inauguration, hours after promising to "preserve, protect and defend the Constitution of the United States," he issued pardons and commuted the sentences of the January 6 insurrectionists who had so violently attacked the Capitol and attempted to interfere with the certification of Joe Biden's victory in the 2020 presidential election. He then issued a dizzying flurry of memorandums, proclamations, and executive orders that included eliminating federal diversity, equity, and inclusion (DEI) programs; launching mass deportations of hardworking people who are our neighbors and who are central to the American economy; halting development aid to foreign countries; attacking transgender people and denying them the right to fight for a country they love; firing thousands of federal workers; freezing federal grants, loans, and other financial assistance and then rescinding the measure, causing widespread chaos, even undermining our ability to respond collectively as one nation in the wake of natural disasters through FEMA, while he and his allies in Congress put in place policies that are hastening climate change and the coming of more destructive and more frequent storms. He turned his back on the allies who had stood with America to protect liberal democracy for the past eighty years. He bowed the knee to dictators with no sense of human rights or human dignity. He issued a flurry of tariffs that will weaken the American economy and our standing in the world. He weaponized the federal government against us by deploying the National Guard and a larger, well-financed, poorly trained, and radicalized version of ICE to our streets engaged in profiling as a matter of daily practice and other illegal, brutal, and sometimes deadly tactics against noncitizens and citizens alike. This is Trump's divided America.

These days have left us all feeling overwhelmed, hurt, confused, but we know where to turn for strength: *Lord, help!*

Healing the country will be a monumental work. I suspect we are all traumatized in ways that we may not fully appreciate. The preacher is no exception. I sometimes think maybe America can't help itself. Every time it seems that we might have a reckoning with our past, it turns out that we can't quite muster up the will to do it after all. When George Floyd was murdered, we saw a plethora of companies, institutions, banks, and universities lining up to ask how they could help. But that help never fully materialized. Now we're seeing an out-and-out assault on any effort that seeks inclusion; a war on women, especially black women; a war on higher education; and an attack on small-business owners.

Some look at the enormity of our divisions and wonder if the struggle is worth it. They ask, "Should I just give up on America?" But that's not possible. At least, not for me. I choose not to leave, physically, mentally, or emotionally. America is my home. My ancestors helped build this country at a time when the Constitution did not even recognize them as fully human. They fought and died in wars against our foreign enemies, even as the powers that be warred against them at home. They endured great suffering for every millimeter of progress. Right here.

Like us, the people of ancient Israel shared a longing for a familiar past and what was once home. And while some of them eventually returned, I submit that the thrust of Isaiah's message is not so much about a return as it is about a reimagining. There is a profound way in which none of us can ever return to what was. That is true notwithstanding the protestations of those who proffer a politics of nostalgia. All too often, that troubling yearning for an idyllic, imagined past conveniently ignores those who were never embraced from the beginning. Given our beloved country's long history of slavery, segregation, and subjugation, what could it possibly mean for people of color, women, and members of the LGBTQ+ community to "make America great again"? Is it truly possible, even desirable, to return?

I am drawn to Isaiah, not only because of his righteous anger but also because he manages to transmit hope, even in such harsh and chaotic times. His hope proceeds from the knowledge that, as difficult as it sometimes may be to believe, we are not alone in this world. We are not hapless orphans abandoned on the doorstep of destiny. God has not forgotten us. Rather, we are called to collaborate with the Creator and with one another, building together a new future that edges us closer to God's dream for humanity. There is a promise and a comfort in his vision of absolute transformation, and his are principles that speak to us all because they're universal. They are resonant in *all* faith traditions, as well as with people of moral courage who claim no particular religion or faith at all. Regardless of how we choose to define our beliefs, we all share a basic human longing for purpose and connection that transcends our own narrow self-interest.

My hope is that this book will energize and encourage you to take a spiritual journey with me across six key issues facing us as Americans today. Viewing them through the clarifying lens of Isaiah's moral topography, I zero in on these six crises because each represents a moral flash point at the center of our politics and the current culture wars in America. Each occupies enormous space and thought and suffering in our collective dynamic: *voting rights and voter suppression*, *the growing influence of dark money*, *the persistence of poverty*, *mass incarceration*, *gun violence*, and *the climate emergency*.

Most of us would agree that resolving these six pressing crises is central to our survival, and yet our politics and collective culture are so poisoned, we have a long way to go before resolving them. I will walk through each explosive topic as a pastor of Ebenezer Baptist Church, where Dr. King served, as a parent of two young children, and as a U.S. senator from Georgia. This conversation is so desperately needed at this historical moment. If we continue to view each of these urgent crises strictly through a partisan, political lens, we will find little or no common ground, and the problems that perplex us will never get solved. The noise and strife of twenty-four-hour news cycles and of bitterly divisive elections only encourage us to drift further away from the sacred covenant we share with one another.

We have reduced the conversation about America's future to partisan politics and nothing else. And while that screaming match has gotten louder and louder, our vision has gotten smaller and smaller. The voices of the people have become increasingly marginalized in their own house. We're discussing polling when we should be discussing policy, and the media cover the elections like the playoffs. Which politician is winning, which is losing? Who's up, who's down? Who's in, who's out? Who cares?! We have forgotten the fundamental truth that we are an American people "tied in a single garment of destiny," as Dr. King put it. Our vast political differences notwithstanding, we need one another.

But will we have the moral fortitude to build on the work done by the great but imperfect patriots who preceded us? Will we have the stamina to continue building, brick by brick, an America of the people, by the people, and for the people? Or will the desires of a greedy few continue to dominate our national discourse, distorting the wants and needs of the many and rendering the rest of us without voice or vote?

The timing of this book is pivotal. This miracle called America, our home, turns 250 years old on July 4, 2026. This date also marks the two hundredth anniversary of the death of Thomas Jefferson, a founding father, the primary author of the Declaration of Independence, and our nation's third president. Perhaps no one embodies the paradox that is America more than Jefferson, who made freedom, liberty, and equality the centerpiece of the new nation's democracy, even as he kept hundreds of people enslaved and fathered children with one of them.

Traditionally, Jefferson's last words are remembered as "Is

it the Fourth?" In a sense, it is a question we are still asking: Has America delivered on its promises yet? For the abolitionist leader Frederick Douglass in his time, the answer was "not yet." As he wrote in 1852 in "What to the Slave Is the Fourth of July?": "The blessings in which you, this day, rejoice, are not enjoyed in common. The rich inheritance of justice, liberty, prosperity and independence, bequeathed by your fathers, is shared by you, not by me. The sunlight that brought light and healing to you, has brought stripes and death to me. This Fourth of July is yours, not mine."

To the descendants of the enslaved, Juneteenth, the celebration that marks when the last of the enslaved people in Texas finally learned that they were free two years after the Emancipation Proclamation, is the day of rejoicing. The day of liberation, freedom, and hope. The promise of our ever-evolving America, a grand cathedral that remains under construction.

As imperfect as he was, Jefferson possessed an enduring vision that was broad and beautiful enough to behold what America *could* become. Yet for those ideals of liberty and justice for all—ideals that Jefferson himself deeply etched in the Declaration of Independence, ideals beyond even his human frailties—to live, to become fully realized, some things had to die. Old thoughts. Old ways. Old laws.

Today, the preeminent question is, which America do we

want to be? Now is the time when we must clarify and redefine our shared values and make an urgent choice. Do we have the will to build what Dr. Martin Luther King Jr. called the "beloved community"? When it comes to providing equal opportunity, creating a democracy where every citizen has a voice, eliminating mass incarceration, making public spaces safe from indiscriminate gun violence, and healing the planet, we suffer not from a paucity of resources but from a poverty of moral imagination.

Will we give in, through either active support or passive resignation, to the demagogues who seek to divide us? Or will we stand up for the best in the American covenant? I am calling for a more inclusive kind of faith. Faith in ourselves as an American people. Faith in the basic goodness of our neighbors. Faith in the ongoing, perfecting work of a democracy. I am asking us to take the long view, to sense the ways in which the cries of our children and the writhing of a planet in peril summon us to a grander and nobler moral vision.

The stakes could not be higher. We could lose our democracy. We could lose our planet. We could lose our souls. We must choose the path we will take carefully, wisely, with our whole selves—minds, bodies, and souls. In these painful and perilous times, I am a man of faith calling on all of us to believe in this vision of a shared future, a community wide and spacious enough for all of us. After all, I am not a senator who used to be a pastor. I am a pastor who serves in the Senate.

Putting forth Isaiah's moral vision for a deeply divided American people standing at a crossroads, I ask the country to choose our better selves and our highest ideals. I ask us to do the hard, collective work that we must thoughtfully and faithfully do. To be sure, this is not a how-to book for political activism or policy. How that will look will be different for each individual. But each of us must decide that a country with such a complicated and tortured history still *can* rightly think of itself as an inclusive family capable of working together to create a desired future.

I hope this book will engage all our American family—people of all faiths and stripes and political persuasions. I hope the teachings of Isaiah will strike a collective chord within each of us, one that quickens the pace of change and inspires us to envision a wide and robust view of the future like none we've ever before imagined.

This book has three central goals. One, I aim to inspire us to renew the covenant that we have with one another, to talk to people outside of our comfort zone, and to do this regularly and more intentionally. Two, I urge those of us in politics to take an extended view beyond election cycles and to start focusing on the needs of the people we purportedly serve, rather than our own ambitions. And three, I encourage those who are currently so disillusioned, checked out, and fed up that they are understandably indifferent to the noise of politics and politicians to get back involved, roll up their sleeves, and reengage in building the kind of America that is worthy of our most precious resource, our children. All our children.

The work is not easy. It is often messy, laborious, loud. And achieving the greatness that is possible takes a long time. But the grand cathedral that we call America is worth our best efforts. So we keep building.

THE CROOKED PLACES MADE STRAIGHT

1

A SPARK OF THE DIVINE

This is what the Lord says: "Maintain justice and do what is right, for my salvation is close at hand and my righteousness will soon be revealed." (Isaiah 56:1, NIV)

On January 5, 2021, Georgia voters did an amazing thing. In a contentious and historic runoff election, they chose me as Georgia's first African American senator and the first black Democrat from the South ever to serve in the U.S. Senate. It was an honor for me and a monumental victory for a region that still holds so many painful vestiges of slavery, discrimination, and racial oppression. During that same runoff, in another historic win, my counterpart and brother, Jon Ossoff, the son of an immigrant, was elected as the first Jewish senator to represent Georgia. Together, we flipped a red state in the old Confederacy, becoming the first Georgia

Democrats to be sent to the Senate in twenty years. A century prior, Georgia had been represented in the U.S. Senate by noted racist and anti-Semite Thomas Watson.

Ossoff's and my victories were more than symbolic. With the Senate now divided 50–50 along party lines, our two seats, together with the tie-breaking vote of Vice President Kamala Harris—the first Asian, the first African American, and the first woman to serve in that high office—gave Democrats an effective majority.

This was my America, I thought to myself proudly in the early morning hours of January 6. My then-eighty-two-year-old mother, who picked cotton as a teenager in Waycross, Georgia, had joined with others in record-breaking voter turnout. For me, an enduring image from that day was of her hands, which had once picked somebody else's cotton, picking her youngest son to be a U.S. senator. My father, a patriotic U.S. Army veteran, small-business entrepreneur, and holiness preacher who lifted abandoned cars on weekdays and lifted broken people on weekends, did not live to see this day. He had died more than a decade earlier at age ninety-three. But I could feel his pride as I became only the eleventh black senator in American history. In the heart of old Dixie, in the place where my dad, as a young soldier in uniform, once had been forced to give up his seat on a bus to a white teenager, it seemed that an emerging multiracial majority was leading the country. The country seemed to be tiptoeing toward our highest and noblest ideals. With my chest puffed out and my head held high, I was so very proud of this new emerging South and of what we'd accomplished as a nation. That morning, *Morning Joe*, *Good Morning America*, and other morning news programs invited me onto their shows to talk about the monumental change we had achieved. With a sly smile, I announced to my friends and family that I knew I had arrived because I was on *The View* talking to Whoopi Goldberg!

But my victory lap was short-lived. By lunchtime my phone began to buzz with alerts. Something terrible was happening at the Capitol building. We all know what came next. In the early afternoon of January 6, the other side of our complicated American family story emerged. The ugly side. Goaded by President Donald Trump, a violent mob of more than two thousand people descended upon the U.S. Capitol hoping to stop the count of the electoral votes that would certify Joe Biden as winner of the 2020 presidential election. They breached perimeters, stormed the building, and assaulted some 170 Metropolitan and Capitol Police officers. Outside, they had built gallows with a noose, and they called for the hanging of Vice President Mike Pence. They desecrated the people's house, vandalizing and looting offices, breaking windows and furniture, and smearing human excrement on the walls. They terrorized civil servants, staffers, and lawmakers, who were forced to take shelter in undisclosed locations. Their involvement in an attempted coup led, directly or indirectly, to the deaths of at least nine people.

Pundits and observers of that fateful day often dismiss the mob as political and social outliers. "That's not who we are as a country," they say. That may sound good and feel good, but I disagree. If we're honest, January 6 is exactly who we are, and who we have always been. Here's the thing. Like all families, our America is complicated. Our beloved country is both the hope of January 5 and the horror of January 6. Both the miracle of democracy and the oppression that runs counter to democracy are right there in our charter documents. Our Declaration of Independence, our Constitution, and our Bill of Rights are all evidence of the enormous possibilities we represent, as well as of our brutal human flaws and failures. Both days are at the very core of who we are, and who we might yet become. The continuing struggle for people of goodwill in this country must be to help push this nation closer to the hope of January 5. As once stated by the Russian author and dissident Aleksandr Solzhenitsyn, "The line separating good and evil runs through the heart of every man." Maimonides puts it this way: "The universe is equally balanced between good and evil. . . . Your next move will tip the scale." I ask, what will be America's next move?

If we are honest, over the last couple years, we have moved closer to the politics of January 6 than January 5. After all, the insurrectionist president was elected to a second term. And in one of his first official acts, he issued pardons for all the nearly 1,600 mob members charged or convicted with crimes connected to the attack on the Capitol, including those who assaulted police officers. Trump even commuted the sentences of fourteen militia members who had been charged with seditious conspiracy. Since his election, there has been an unabashed and unrelenting assault on the hard-fought progress that has finally made it possible for someone like me to serve in the U.S. Senate.

Our progress toward the hope of January 5 is fragile. At this point, a whopping fourteen black people, five of them black women, have had the title of United States senator since the nation's founding 250 years ago! To date, out of more than two thousand senators, only sixty-four have been women! Because this kind of progress in government, corporate, and other spaces is apparently too much to bear, Trump and his allies have succeeded in making the very idea of diversity, equity, and inclusion radical, controversial, and in some cases illegal. In a nation of immigrants, immigrants—both undocumented and legal—have been subjected to organized cruelty and rendered unsafe. The cords that hold us as one people united in our vast diversity are frayed, and the common ground we sometimes take for granted, increasingly fraught.

We are in a rough place right now, fighting to save our fragile democracy. As a man of faith, I often say that I believe democracy is the political enactment of a spiritual idea. It is the notion that each of us has within us a spark of the divine. Therefore, we ought to have a vote and a voice in the direction of our country and our destiny within it. One person, one vote. This revolutionary idea of self-governance is rare, precious, more the exception than the rule throughout world history. The rank authoritarianism that created so much repression, destruction, and devastation in the twentieth century has come raging back like a mutant strain of a deadly virus in the twenty-first. The story of that fight is being written in real time, ironically as our nation celebrates the 250th anniversary of this grand experiment. The outcome cannot be taken for granted.

In a journal kept by James McHenry, a Maryland delegate to the Constitutional Convention in 1787, McHenry recounts a story about the last day of the convention when a woman from Philadelphia asked Benjamin Franklin, a convention delegate and governor of Pennsylvania, an important question about the new system of governance.

She asked, "Well, Doctor, what have we got, a republic or a monarchy?"

"A republic," he replied, referring to a government in which people elect their leaders. "If you can keep it."

If you can keep it.

In response to that daunting challenge, I have often found myself praying, "Lord, help!" But if we are inclined to pray, we must pray with our lips and our legs, our hands and our feet. There is an old West African proverb that says, "When you pray, move your feet." Ours is the world's oldest and greatest democratic republic. But great patriots have always had to move their feet—to stand and fight to win it, to keep it and to expand the meaning of its promise. It was the movement of feet at the Battle of Saratoga that began to turn the tide for American troops in their valiant fight for freedom, convincing them that they could indeed be victorious in the struggle against the tyranny of the British. Harriet Tubman, a deeply spiritual and prayerful woman, moved her feet to secure not only her own freedom but also the freedom of some seventy other enslaved persons during thirteen incredibly dangerous missions to the South. With an eloquence consecrated by principled action, William Lloyd Garrison, Frederick Douglass, Harriet

Beecher Stowe, and other abolitionists moved their feet, a president, and a nation toward emancipating itself from the ugly contradiction of slavery. The stories of women's suffrage, civil rights, and the dignity and inclusion of the disabled as well as the LGBTQ+ community standing up at Stonewall are all chapters inked in the blood, sweat, and tears of citizens who dared to move their feet. They understood, like Benjamin Franklin, that it is a republic if you can keep it.

In other words, if we are not careful, we could lose the very thing that makes us America. After all, our democratic republic—a nation represented by a government "of the people, by the people, for the people"—is a decided departure from most of human history. It is clear from the story that McHenry shared in his journal, which is housed at the Library of Congress, that those who laid out the grand vision for this nation recognized from the beginning that democracy is vulnerable to the whims of those who are hungry for power, who wish to squeeze out the voices of the people and rule over them.

There is built-in protection, though: freedom of speech, even speech that criticizes the government; freedom of religion; the right of assembly; equal protection under the law; checks and balances of power preserved by three *coequal* branches of government. And all of this is facilitated and maintained by the right of individual citizens to vote. Thus, the protection of our democracy hinges on voting rights, because the right to vote is preservative of all other rights. That fight drew thousands of women into the streets of the nation's capital on March 3, 1913, for a historic demonstration calling for a constitutional amendment that would guarantee women the right to vote—an amendment that would take another six years to win congressional approval. That fight led Medgar Evers, the NAACP's first field secretary in Mississippi, to travel throughout the state, registering and organizing black voters—activity considered so threatening that a white supremacist murdered him in his driveway on June 12, 1963. That fight drew African Americans and their supporters of all races to the Edmund Pettus Bridge in Selma, Alabama, in March 1965, for a series of marches, including one brutal day that became known as Bloody Sunday.

That day was March 7, 1965, and John Lewis was just twenty-five years old when he and other civil rights activists led about six hundred marchers across the bridge on what began as a fifty-four-mile journey on foot from Selma to Montgomery, the Alabama state capital, to push for voting rights. But local police and state troopers, some on horseback, were waiting with tear gas canisters, billy clubs, and cattle prods to stop their progress. We've seen the black-and-white photos and grainy television news footage of the officers' vicious attack on the marchers. Lewis was beaten so badly he had to be hospitalized; an iconic photo shows him on his knees as a state trooper swings a billy club toward his head. Images of the violence unleashed on the peaceful marchers shocked the nation.

Lewis would become one of the heroes of the movement, and he would never lose his fire for voting rights. His presence and the suffering he endured on Bloody Sunday to make voting a possibility for future generations always loomed large many years later when, as his pastor, I had the honor of leading Sunday "Souls to the Polls" bus rides with him through Atlanta during election season. Bloody Sunday was a shameful but pivotal moment that ultimately pushed Congress to pass the Voting Rights Act of 1965, outlawing discriminatory practices, such as poll taxes and literacy tests, aimed at disenfranchising black voters. Consider this! In the five years after its passage, almost as many black voters registered in Alabama, Mississippi, Georgia, Louisiana, North Carolina, and South Carolina as in the entire century before 1965, according to U.S. Justice Department estimates.

For nearly fifty years, that towering federal legislation provided significant voting rights protection. But a precipitous slide backward began in 2013, when the U.S. Supreme Court gutted sections of the Voting Rights Act that required states and jurisdictions with a history of discriminatory practices to get preclearance from the U.S. Justice Department before changing any voting policies. In *Shelby County v. Holder*, the high court's conservative majority struck down the formula in section 4 of the Voting Rights Act that determined which states and localities were required to get prior approval. The ruling essentially ended the preclearance requirement and opened the floodgates for a torrent of voter suppression measures. Justice Ruth Bader Ginsburg wrote in a powerful dissent that "throwing out preclearance when it has worked and is continuing to work to stop discriminatory changes is like throwing away your umbrella in a rainstorm because you are not getting wet." Her words proved to be prophetic.

On the same day as the *Shelby* ruling, Texas state officials announced they would implement a law with a strict photo identification requirement that had been blocked previously in the preclearance process. The law listed seven acceptable forms of identification—a Texas driver's license, state personal identification card, state license to carry a handgun, U.S. military identification card, U.S. citizenship certificate, U.S. passport, or Texas election identification certificate. These IDs were acceptable only if they included a photograph; they also needed to be current, not expired. It was one of the strictest voter identification laws in the country, and the list of acceptable forms of identification was the shortest of any state. After years of court challenges, the measure eventually was struck down by a federal appeals court, which found the Texas law discriminatory against the state's black and Latino citizens. But vicious voter suppression efforts have continued nationwide, even targeting activists who have the audacity to help give poor, poorly educated citizens a voice at the polls.

That's exactly what happened to a group of twelve people in Quitman, Georgia. All but one in the group were black women, and they had the unmitigated audacity to believe they should channel their electoral strength into better representation on a majority-white school board that had not been sensitive to the needs of their community's children. They organized themselves and flipped the board. But soon thereafter, they found themselves facing 120 felony counts of voter fraud and collectively hundreds of years in prison. The shocking story of the group that came to be known as the Quitman 10+2 reads like something out of the 1950s, but this happened in 2010, even before the *Shelby* ruling.

Nancy Dennard was living in Quitman and working as an educator in the Brooks County school system when she first decided to run for the school board in 2004. It seemed to her that some members of the majority-white board were more concerned about blocking property tax increases than about providing needed resources for the majority-black school district. (The county itself was 60 percent white, but public schools were majority black.) But Dennard lost the race in 2004 and then again in 2008. When a special election was held in 2009 to fill a vacancy on the board, she campaigned differently this time, using a strategy that had been employed mostly by Georgia Republicans in recent elections: the absentee ballot. The state legislature, with its Republican majority at the time, had made voting by absentee ballot easier for voters. Dennard won. Meanwhile, complaints by local officials about the large number of absentee ballots that had helped push Dennard to victory had been flowing into the secretary of state's office, which did a cursory investigation but took no action against Dennard.

The next year, buoyed by her own victory, Dennard encouraged Diane Thomas, a middle school math teacher, and Linda Troutman, a longtime educator, both African American, to run for open seats on the board and instructed them on the absentee ballot process and pertinent laws. A troop of relatives and friends joined the campaigns. These organizers significantly increased black voter turnout, and both Thomas and Troutman won in the primary and general elections, flipping the school board from majority white to majority black for the very first time.

Rumors spread through the small town like wildfire. By then, a new secretary of state, Brian Kemp, had taken office and authorized the Georgia Bureau of Investigation to investigate the rumors and complaints of voter fraud. Six weeks after the general election, on December 21, 2010, these women and seven of their volunteers were arrested and accused of voter fraud. Humiliating mug shots of these proud, hardworking folks in orange prison jumpsuits were plastered across the front of the local newspaper and broadcast on local news and eventually on Fox News, as well. Outraged by what seemed an overzealous attempt to punish the women for their victory, their supporters began calling the group the Quitman 10. A year later, two more women were arrested and added to the case, which became known as the Quitman 10+2; a total of 120 felony charges were filed against them. One woman, for example, was charged with 25 counts of "unlawful possession of ballots" and seven counts of "interfering with an elector." Every person charged faced at least twenty years in prison; given their ages, some of them feared spending the rest of their lives in prison.

For years, these citizens' lives were turned upside down as they fought to prove their innocence. Dennard, Troutman, and Thomas were stripped of their school board titles, but a year later the state was forced by law to reinstate them. They turned down offers of plea deals and trusted that they would be vindicated fully someday. One woman died before getting a chance to clear her name. Another woman, Lula Smart, Thomas's sister, became so depressed that she wanted to die. Smart went to trial three times, since the first two ended in mistrials. The third time, in September 2014, a jury found her not guilty on all counts. She was the only one of the group who went to trial. Three months after Smart was acquitted, all remaining charges were dropped against the other members. Their vindication took four long years.

Even after all they went through, some members of the Quitman 10+2 remained devoted public servants. Smart would go on to win a seat on the county commission in 2015. Dennard left the school board to run for mayor in 2017 and won. And Thomas, who had lost a previous reelection bid for the school board, ran for Dennard's seat in 2016 and won.

Years later, while traveling through Georgia during my reelection campaign in 2022, I stopped in Quitman to meet voters and had the chance to meet some of those courageous women. I recall traveling far off the beaten path to a white building filled with people. They gave me a warm hero's welcome, and I felt a bit embarrassed because they were the true heroes. Dr. Nancy Dennard, whose brilliance had changed things forever in her hometown, introduced me. Gratitude rose from the depths of my soul as I thought about the injustice she and her comrades had endured and how the community of people gathered before me had stood with them. I stood there for a moment and just looked at them.

"I have longed to be with you," I began, tears welling in my eyes.

When I think of the Quitman case and other efforts across the nation to suppress the vote and weaken the power of the minority voter, I'm reminded of Ben Franklin's warning about the fragility of our democracy. *If you can keep it.*

Unfortunately, the Quitman case would be just the beginning for Secretary of State Kemp, who would continue his voter suppression efforts. But he was not alone. Voter suppression policies metastasized throughout this country with Trump's false claims of election fraud when he was defeated by Joe Biden in 2020. After insurrectionists stormed the Capitol building in a failed attempt to halt the certification of a free and fair election, Republican state lawmakers in over two dozen states got busy, dismantling the progress of generations by pushing through a phalanx of voter suppression laws. In Georgia, for example, the Republican majority passed Senate Bill 202, which made sweeping changes to the state's election laws. Governor Brian Kemp—the same Kemp who as secretary of state had presided over the investigations into the Quitman 10+2—signed the measure into law as the so-called Election Integrity Act. There is no integrity in a law that disenfranchises voters.

A record number of Georgians had voted by mail during my first election, and so Senate Bill 202 made the process more difficult by cutting in half the period in which voters could request absentee ballots (from about six months to less than three). At the same time, the law reduced the number of drop boxes to return the ballots and mandated that the boxes be moved inside government buildings and early-voting centers, which were open only during business hours. That mandate essentially eliminated the previous twenty-four-hour access for workers who needed to take advantage of early-morning or late-night drop-offs to cast their votes. Additionally, the statute made it against the law for elected officials to mail absentee ballots to all voters before an election, as had been done in prior election years, and the law added strict new voter identification requirements for absentee ballots. The legislators' focus on absentee voting was relentless.

The law also required the Georgia attorney general's office to operate an election hotline and investigate complaints from any caller reporting suspected voter fraud. On its face that might not sound so bad, but what that mandate really did was enable any random voter to make unlimited, frivolous mass challenges to the eligibility of other voters registered in their county. In 2022, just six right-wing activists challenged the voter registrations of 89,000 Georgia voters. Let that sink in. Of the 100,000 voter challenges that year, 89,000 of them came from six right-wing activists.

In addition, Senate Bill 202 reduced the advance voting period for runoffs from three weeks to one week, with no mandatory weekend voting days, and outlawed mobile voting units unless the governor had declared a natural disaster emergency to allow them. These changes created horrible conditions for many voters, who at certain polling places in the 2020 elections had already reported waiting in line for hours to vote. The good news is that they'd endured it and voted.

To add insult to the indefensible conditions Senate Bill 202 caused, the measure also banned any non–poll worker from providing food or water to those waiting in line. Violators would face misdemeanor charges. This feature of the law made it into national news reports, drew outrage from all over the country, and was challenged in court—and I understand why. But it seems to me that we ought to be asking a more fundamental question. With all our technology, resources, and experience with conducting elections, *why* are some people standing in line so long that they *need* food and water? Who wants lunch or refreshments while simply trying to exercise their constitutional right to vote?

Research tells us that the voting experience for black and Latino voters is vastly different from that of our white brothers and sisters. According to analysis of the 2018 midterm elections by NYU Law's Brennan Center for Justice, a nonpartisan law and policy institute, black voters nationwide waited 45 percent longer in line to vote on average than white voters; Latino voters waited 46 percent longer. In the 2020 primary election, some black voters in Fulton County reported waiting longer than five hours to vote, and during early voting in the 2020 general election, some Cobb County voters waited more than ten hours to cast their ballots, according to news reports.

The crux of the problem is this: The number of registered voters in Georgia has exploded by nearly two million people since the *Shelby* decision in 2013, while polling locations had been cut throughout the state by nearly 10 percent, according to an analysis of state and local records by Georgia Public Broadcasting and *ProPublica*. And those new voters tended to be younger and nonwhite, especially in nine metro Atlanta counties. Nationally, the racial voter turnout gap had been widening since the *Shelby* decision. Strikingly, in areas previously under a preclearance requirement, that gap had grown twice as fast. The Supreme Court decision moved us backward, not forward, in the long march to secure and broaden participation in the most fundamental right of a democracy.

That is why I was concerned in November 2022, during my own U.S. Senate runoff, when Georgia's secretary of state, Brad Raffensperger, claimed state law prevents voting on the second Saturday before an election if there is a holiday on the preceding Thursday or Friday. The cited holidays were Thanksgiving and the following Friday, which is an unnamed paid state holiday that had been set aside to observe Confederate General Robert E. Lee's birthday. In 2015, then–Georgia Governor Nathan Deal, a Republican, removed Lee's name from the holiday but kept the day as a paid holiday for state employees. The quiet change came just weeks after a twenty-one-year-old admitted white supremacist joined a Bible study group at Emanuel African Methodist Episcopal Church in Charleston, South Carolina, and then took out a gun and shot to death nine members of the congregation, who had welcomed him warmly. The murders renewed intense debate throughout the South over Confederate monuments and observances.

My campaign had drawn broad support from young people of all races and ethnicities, including many college students returning to Georgia for the Thanksgiving holidays. Preventing voting that Saturday would have blocked the votes of countless college students, as well as working-class citizens who punch the clock during the week and cannot afford to lose pay while standing in long lines at the polls. I am certain that Republican officials had analyzed my first win with surgical precision, so it would have come as no surprise to them that this move would hurt my campaign.

Voter suppression is about shaving off a few votes here and a few votes there, which in tight races can make all the difference. In 2018, the secretary of state's office, still led by Kemp at the time, suspended the applications of about fifty-three thousand voters, most of whom were black. The office claimed the voter registration forms contained discrepancies, such as information on the form not exactly matching that on a driver's license or a

Social Security card. In his race for governor that year, Kemp narrowly defeated my friend Stacey Abrams, an attorney, a former Georgia state representative, and a voting rights activist, by about fifty-five thousand votes. Those suspended votes mattered.

"Voter suppression isn't only about blocking the vote," Abrams said during her gubernatorial debate against Kemp. "It's also about creating an atmosphere of fear, making people worry that their votes won't count."

I saw this firsthand.

So when the secretary of state's office attempted to ban voting on that Thanksgiving weekend, I knew I had to take a stand. I sued the state. My legal team argued that the law was being misinterpreted and did not apply to the runoff, and we won. The state appealed; we won again when the court refused the state's request to halt the lower court ruling. Three Republican committees then petitioned the Georgia Supreme Court for emergency relief. I wondered, relief from whom? The people? Voters? We won again; the court rejected their petition. More than seventy thousand people voted on the weekend in question. My margin of victory in that race was not that much more, 99,389 votes. Every vote matters.

Voting is such a sacred, noble right. One person. One vote.

Long before I considered running for public office, I was working to register voters and fighting to protect voting rights. I relish the memories of sitting next to my parishioner and mentor John R. Lewis and Christine King Farris, Dr. King's big sister, on the bus, headed to vote with our fellow congregants during the church's Souls to the Polls campaign. Even that purposeful activity was threatened by changes rendered by SB 202. As I said in my maiden speech on the floor of the U.S. Senate, we are witnessing a massive and unabashed assault on voting rights unlike anything we have seen since the Jim Crow era. He's back, wearing new clothes, threatening to topple our democracy. Our democracy is only as strong as our will to fight for it.

If we can keep it.

Another issue that I believe silences the voices of everyday Americans is gerrymandering, when state legislatures manipulate the redrawing of district maps in state and federal elections for partisan or racial purposes. Redistricting, as the process is called, occurs every ten years, when states are required to redraw their congressional and state legislative boundaries to reflect population changes revealed by the census. In most states, state legislatures are responsible for this process. In the remaining, districts are redrawn by independent commissions, courts, or political commissions with members from both parties. As Republicans have gained greater control of state legislatures across the country, they have drawn maps to protect themselves and dilute the voting power of people of color, who typically vote for Democrats. Like the overwhelming influence of dark money in our federal elections and politics, gerrymandering, too, is a major threat to our democracy. It often results in the disenfranchisement of voters, particularly black and Hispanic voters, who are so spread out across these gerrymandered districts that their votes have little impact on who gets elected to represent them.

Former U.S. Attorney General Eric Holder is doing important work in this area as chairman of the National Democratic Redistricting Committee, which has had some success battling gerrymandered districts in Republican-led states at the U.S. Supreme Court. In 2021 and 2022, the Redistricting Committee initiated lawsuits in Alabama and Louisiana on behalf of black voters who were being disenfranchised. In both states, legislators redrew congressional district boundaries after the 2020 census and created just one majority-black district that gave black voters in each state an opportunity to elect a representative of their choice. Based on the 2020 census, black voters make up nearly a third of the population in both states. However, black voters were so scattered throughout the remaining majority-white congressional districts that their votes would have little impact, given both states' racially polarized voting patterns. The Redistricting Committee and other civil rights organizations argued that the dilution of the black vote violated section 2 of the Voting Rights Act, which bans racially discriminatory voting policies. In 2023, the U.S.

Supreme Court, even with its conservative majority, sided with black voters in the Alabama case, *Allen v. Milligan*, ruling that Alabama's redistricting map likely violates section 2 of the Voting Rights Act. The case returned to Alabama for resolution, and while the legislators there have been defiant, a federal court has ordered the use of an independently drawn congressional map with a second predominantly black district for the remainder of the decade. In Louisiana, the *Allen v. Milligan* ruling prompted legislators to redraw the state's congressional boundaries to also include a second majority-black district.

There are ways that Democrats have cut deals, benefited from gerrymandering, and thus ceded some of the moral high ground on this issue. But as Holder said during an interview on National Public Radio, comparing the small gains Democrats have achieved through gerrymandering to those of Republicans is like comparing "apples to oranges or a really small apple to a very large apple." Either way, he has said—and I concur—it's cheating and deprives American citizens of the right to help elect those who will represent their policy desires. Holder describes gerrymandering as "the biggest rigged system in America." It is how you get a Marjorie Taylor Greene, the caustic, extreme right-wing U.S. representative from northwest Georgia. There are very few congressional races in our country that are truly competitive these days. And my concern, as always, is that the voices of ordinary Americans, particularly poor people and people of color, are carved out of the picture.

This became eminently clear in the state of Texas in 2025. At Donald Trump's behest and in advance of the 2026 midterm elections, Republicans in the Texas legislature designed what some describe as the most racially gerrymandered map in the state's history since 1965, the year the Voting Rights Act was passed into law. This they did in the middle of the decade, although reapportionment typically happens every ten years, following the census, and also while saying the quiet part out loud: that their goal was to make it difficult for Democrats to win. These tactics are not new, but as the Texas situation and the ensuing debacle make clear, they are used with abandon without the necessary voter protections that have given a truly inclusive democracy a fighting chance in the years since the civil rights movement.

That is why I came to Congress fighting for voting rights. Voting rights are the foundation and the framework in which we get to fight for all the things that matter. That is why I used my initial Senate speech to urge my colleagues to support the John R. Lewis Voting Rights Advancement Act of 2021, which had been named to pay tribute to the man who had served honorably in Congress for more than three decades until his death in 2020. He had put his body on the line during the civil rights movement to push our nation to live up to its ideals.

The measure proposed to restore the full protections of the 1965 Voting Rights Act, namely by reinstating the preclearance provision and establishing new criteria for determining which states and jurisdictions would need preapproval by the U.S. Justice Department before changing laws that impact voting rights. When the Supreme Court struck down the provision in 2013, justices called the preclearance formula outdated and suggested that Congress establish a new one, reflective of current conditions. But federal legislators have been unable to agree on a new formula.

A companion bill, the For the People Act of 2021, was also introduced, and one of my first acts as a U.S. senator was to sign on as a proud cosponsor. The bill proposed to strengthen voting rights in the following ways: establishing automatic national voter registration for eligible voters when they provide their information to a government agency, like the Department of Motor Vehicles; allowing all Americans to register to vote online and on Election Day; requiring states to have two weeks of early voting, including weekends, in federal elections; protecting programs like Souls to the Polls; prohibiting states from restricting absentee voting; stopping widespread voter purging based on unreliable evidence, such as a person's voting history; ending the dominance of big money in politics; and more.

The John R. Lewis Voting Rights Advancement Act passed the House but failed to get enough votes to pass the Senate. The bill received unified support from Democrats in the Senate, but Republicans blocked it and also its companion bill with a filibuster.

It seems so long ago that the Voting Rights Act won bipartisan support. Legislators of both parties seemed to recognize the significant role that protecting the precious right to vote plays in protecting our democracy. The last time Congress approved amendments to the Voting Rights Act was 2006 under Republican President George W. Bush. The measure passed by a vote of 98–0 in the Senate. But those days seem long gone.

We are in a rough place. Nevertheless, we must fight undeterred to make the rough places smooth and the crooked places straight.

That is why, in March 2024, I joined several of my colleagues in reintroducing the John R. Lewis Voting Rights Advancement Act. "This legislation is more important than ever, because the fight to protect voting rights and voting access for every eligible American remains unfinished," I told my colleagues. "And even worse, so much of the progress Congressman Lewis fought for is being rolled back."

While recognizing that fact, we must not allow it to discourage us or dissuade us from the fight. That fight is sacred. So I have continued to fight, introducing the bill again in July 2025. I refuse to give up. The stakes are too high. The vote is the call-and-response of citizens gathered together in the grand cathedral of our democracy. It is a kind of prayer for the world we desire for ourselves and our children. We must continue praying with our lips and our legs, our hands and our feet, because progress is hard-fought, and in America it has always come in fits and starts. There are times when democracy's promise of "justice for *all*" expands and times when it contracts. Contractions are painful, but they create the conditions for new birth. May we learn the lessons of the last few years and find the strength to dig deep and push toward a brighter and more inclusive America. In our movement is a spark of the divine. May we find it, and may it strengthen us to push and press on.

2

SQUEEZING OUT "THE LEAST OF THESE"

Who really owns our democracy? Is it secretly for sale to the highest bidder?

In January 2010, the nation's highest court seemed to answer that question in the affirmative when it announced its narrow 5–4 decision in the *Citizens United v. Federal Election Commission* case, which upended century-old campaign finance reforms that restricted the amount of money that corporations and other outside groups could spend on political campaigns. The ruling kicked open the doors for corporations and special interest groups to pour as much money as they wished into elections with legal protection. And just as President Obama and other critics of the *Citizens United* decision predicted, millions of corporate dollars began flowing furiously into federal elections, much of it funneled through opaque nonprofit groups, which claimed they were not required to disclose the identities of their donors.

"As a result, the American political system became awash in unlimited, untraceable cash," investigative reporter Jane Mayer wrote in her astonishing 2016 book, aptly titled *Dark Money*. Mayer lays out in convincing detail how a group of billionaire businessmen have pooled their enormous resources for decades to set up a network of right-leaning think tanks, media outlets, and academic programs, and to influence elections and political appointments, dramatically altering the country's political and legal landscape to suit their self-serving, conservative agenda.

As the prophet Isaiah warned during Israel's dark days long ago, when a nation's leaders are corrupt, society's most vulnerable suffer.

> Your rulers are rebels, partners with thieves; they all love bribes and chase after gifts. They do not defend the cause of the fatherless; the widow's case does not come before them. (Isaiah 1:23, NIV)

Who will defend the powerless, those described in Matthew 25 as "the least of these"? In my ministry at Ebenezer Church, we are oriented toward tending to the least of these. Isaiah calls on both religious and political leaders to do the same. I have firsthand experience with what is at stake. As someone who grew up with two hardworking parents but little material wealth, I am ever grateful for the government programs and protections that made it possible for me to have access to a quality education, beginning with Head Start. I was a Head Start baby, and I remain grateful to my God and my country for the early exposure it gave me to the potential for academic excellence as I grew older. That's the same program that my Republican colleagues proposed cutting in the 2025 congressional session, while pushing to give their billionaire buddies tax cuts.

But it's not only Head Start. Federal grants and loans helped to finance my academic journey through Morehouse College. Standing on that firm foundation, I would go on to receive two master's degrees and a PhD from Union Theological Seminary. Later, the kid from the projects and the first college graduate in a large family would be called upon to lead Martin Luther King Jr.'s church! My life in public service is a testament to what is possible when the government lifts up hardworking Americans whose incomes fall short of meeting the substantive needs of their families. But increasingly, I've seen our government tilt away from caring for society's most vulnerable and toward the interests of the financiers who have leveraged their wealth to tear down the protections put in place over time to level the playing field, to give every child a fighting chance. The legal restrictions on campaign finance were aimed at keeping those with money from gaining outsize influence over our elected officials.

But the plan to change the rules of the game was well orchestrated.

In 2008, Citizens United, a conservative nonprofit political advocacy group, released a documentary film called *Hillary: The Movie,* severely criticizing presidential candidate Hillary Clinton. Citizens United planned to broadcast ads to promote the film and pay a cable company to make it available free to subscribers via "video on demand." But federal election law prohibited corporations and labor unions from using their funds to create "electioneering communications," which are defined as any broadcast, cable, or satellite communication that refers to a clearly identified federal candidate within thirty days of a primary election and sixty days of a general election. Citizens United filed a complaint to challenge the constitutionality of the law and ask the U.S. district court to stop the Federal Election Commission from enforcing it.

The founder of Citizens United, Floyd Brown, was well-known in right-wing circles as a political consultant—some might call him a campaign hit man—who specializes in digging up dirt on political opponents, or at least exploiting a sensitive issue in hopes of destroying the opposition's election chances. In 1988, Brown served as political director of Americans for Bush, a Republican-aligned political action committee (PAC) that produced the infamously racist Willie Horton television commercial during George H. W. Bush's presidential campaign. Horton was an African American inmate serving a life sentence in Massachusetts for murder when he was released for a weekend furlough. He escaped and ten months later was caught in Maryland, where he had raped a white woman and stabbed her boyfriend. Brown and his team linked Bush's Democratic opponent, Massachusetts Governor Michael Dukakis, to the furlough program in the television ad, which played on white fear of black criminals and portrayed Dukakis as soft on crime—a label he was not able to shake. As criticism of the race-baiting nature of the ad intensified, Bush's team tried to distance him from it, but the intended damage had been done; the ad helped to sink the Dukakis campaign. But even more, it put Democratic politicians on the defensive for years to come, which arguably led to their support of tough crime laws that disproportionately locked up African Americans. With the 1988 election serving as proof that he was adept in the game of political influence, Brown founded Citizens United.

The district court ruled against Citizens United's complaint against the Federal Election Commission and found that *Hillary: The Movie* was clearly "electioneering communication." Citizens United appealed straight to the Supreme Court, and the high court's expansive landmark decision in January 2010 would shock the nation. The court ruled not only that Citizens United had a right to air the film but also that a limit on independent spending by corporations and special interest groups during elections was unconstitutional because it limited their First Amendment right to free speech. The only time such limits should be allowed, the court said, was to prevent "quid pro quo corruption" such as bribes. Justices who sided with the majority opined that existing disclosure rules would keep election spending transparent and enable voters to assess donors' motives.

The late Justice John Paul Stevens, a registered Republican who often sided with the court's more liberal justices, wrote a long, stinging dissent, distinguishing corporations from individuals and the right of individuals to free speech. "At bottom, the Court's opinion is thus a rejection of the common sense of the American people, who have recognized a need to prevent corporations from undermining self-government since the founding, and who have fought against the distinctive corrupting potential of corporate electioneering since the days of Theodore Roosevelt," he wrote near the end of his opinion. "It is a strange time to repudiate that common sense. While American democracy is imperfect, few outside the majority of this Court would have thought its flaws included a dearth of corporate money in politics."

Justice Stevens was right. American democracy is not intended to facilitate only the pursuit of happiness of the monied corporate class. This is a democracy problem. This is a moral problem. That is because the people's voices have been squeezed out of their democracy. I think of Isaiah 11:4: "But with righteousness he shall judge the poor and decide with equity for the meek of the earth" (ESV).

History had long ago provided a glimpse of the serious threat that big-monied corporations pose to democracy when they secretly try to buy political influence and squeeze out the voices of ordinary people. History already had revealed the crooked places.

The need for campaign finance reform in the first place stemmed from the scandals and the intersection of corporate and political corruption that grew during the late-nineteenth-century industrial boom. Campaign financing was unregulated, and magnates in the railroad, oil, steel, and finance industries leveraged their wealth to try to influence public policy. Mark Hanna, who had made a fortune in the coal, steel, and iron industries, changed the game with his aggressive fundraising approach. He retired from business in 1896 to run the presidential campaign of fellow Ohioan Governor William McKinley. In addition to making a sizable contribution of his own, Hanna solicited significant financial donations from bankers and his industrialist cohorts to help McKinley win the 1896 and 1900 elections. After McKinley's assassination in 1901, Vice President Theodore Roosevelt finished the term and ran for the office in 1904. During that campaign, Roosevelt's Democratic rival accused him of accepting donations from corporations eager to influence his administration—an allegation Roosevelt denied. But the next year, a New York state investigation unwittingly turned up proof with the discovery of a $48,700 contribution that New York Life Insurance had made to the Roosevelt campaign. That campaign contribution would be valued at $1.8 million today.

As the public outcry grew, President Roosevelt, perhaps embarrassed by the scandal, urged Congress to pass campaign finance reform legislation. He ultimately signed into law the Tillman Act of 1907, named for U.S. Senator Benjamin R. Tillman, the South Carolina Democrat (and virulent white supremacist) who introduced the measure, which forbade corporations and interstate banks from contributing to congressional and presidential candidates, as well as political committees. It was the country's first major federal legislation regulating corporate spending in federal elections, and the measure would remain mostly intact for more than a hundred years.

Weak enforcement provisions in the Tillman Act and future scandals would, however, prompt many more election finance regulations. The most comprehensive of these was the Federal Election Campaign Act of 1971, which enacted limits on the amount of monetary and other contributions that could be made to candidates and required campaigns to disclose their expenditures and contributions over $100. Later amendments to the law created the Federal Election Commission to enforce the regulations, enabled corporations and special interest groups to funnel money to campaigns through PACs, and established public financing of presidential campaigns to reduce the reliance on private financing. It seems unimaginable today that in the 1976 presidential race the money spent on both campaigns totaled about $114 million, and about 60 percent of that amount was financed for the first time by public funds. Even if adjusted for inflation to $628 million in 2024, the figure is a far cry from the $3.2 billion raised by 2024 presidential candidates Kamala Harris and Donald Trump and their political parties. That figure does not include another staggering $1.9 billion given by dark-money groups aligned with the Republicans or Democrats to influence the campaign without revealing their donors.

The most recent significant campaign finance reforms occurred in 2002, when Congress passed the Bipartisan Campaign Reform Act, known as the McCain–Feingold Act, in honor of its primary Senate sponsors. This act would prohibit "electioneering communications," political ads supporting or attacking specific federal candidates, within thirty days of a primary and sixty days of a general election—the specific restriction that sparked the *Citizens United* case. But its primary focus was a ban on "soft money," the unlimited (and heretofore unregulated) sums of money that individuals, unions, and special interest groups could send to political parties for so-called party-building activities. Those funds were often used to finance "issue ads," advertisements that indirectly influence campaigns by focusing on a particular political issue rather than a candidate.

Five years earlier, in 1997, amid serious public criticism of the heavy use of soft money in the presidential campaigns of the previous year, a member of one of the Republican Party's wealthiest, most influential donor families spoke up unapologetically about her family's agenda. "I know a little something about soft money, as my family is the largest single contributor of soft money to the national Republican Party," Betsy DeVos wrote in *Roll Call*, a Washington, DC–based newspaper that covers Congress and Capitol Hill. "I have decided, however, to stop taking offense at the suggestion that we are buying influence. Now I simply concede the point. They are right. We do expect some things in return. We expect to foster a conservative governing philosophy consisting of limited government and respect for traditional American virtues. We expect a return on our investment; we expect a good and honest government."

The same year, DeVos became a founding board member of the nonprofit James Madison Center for Free Speech, whose primary mission was to end all legal restrictions on money in politics. In 2017 President Trump gave DeVos a huge seat at the table of influence during his first term by naming her secretary of education—not a bad return on the family's investment.

Crooked places . . .

Contrast this return-on-investment (ROI) theory of influence with Thomas Jefferson's words in the Declaration of Independence: "Governments are instituted among Men, deriving their just powers from the consent of the governed." These days, it can seem like our government is deriving its powers from the highest bidder.

But the James Madison Center was just a cog in the wheel of a much larger political machine aimed at creating a conservative legal system full of judges at every level who are sympathetic to Republican causes. It's no secret around Washington that the main driver of that machine is a conservative activist named Leonard Leo. Leo has created a sprawling network of dark-money groups that for a decade have pushed for the end of campaign finance regulations, affirmative action, abortion rights, antidiscrimination protections, and efforts to slow climate change, as well as for giving state legislatures greater power over federal elections. Leo was spurred into action in 1992, when U.S. Supreme Court Justices Anthony Kennedy, Sandra Day O'Connor, and David Souter, all appointees of Republican presidents, sided with the 5–4 majority in a case upholding the constitutional right to an abortion. Republicans needed a long-term strategy that would cultivate conservative young lawyers and create a pipeline of devotees for spots on the bench, Leo figured.

Leo had just gone to work for the Federalist Society, a legal nonprofit organization founded in 1982 by conservative law students who banded together to combat what they saw as the prevalent liberal ideology being taught in law schools. Over time, Leo became one of the conservative movement's most prolific fundraisers and influencers, and he would build the Federalist Society into a fundraising behemoth and dominant source of conservative jurists. Leo befriended judges, directed law students to clerkships, recommended attorneys for legal jobs in Republican administrations, and ultimately drew up lists of potential federal judges for Republican presidents dating back to George W. Bush (the younger Bush).

Perhaps more than any single person, Leo is credited with building the Supreme Court's supermajority. All six of the current U.S. Supreme Court justices who form that supermajority have been (and some still may be) members or affiliates of the Federalist Society. Though the last three confirmed conservative justices were not yet on the Supreme Court for the *Citizens United* decision in 2010, the case was a big win for the corporate billionaires and multimillion-dollar special interest groups. In one giant swoop, the Supreme Court wiped out many of the campaign finance protections that had taken a century to put in place. The impact has been significant.

The case enabled the creation of super PACs, independent groups that can accept unlimited funds from individuals and corporations as long as the group does not give the funds directly to candidates. A traditional PAC can contribute directly to a candidate's official campaign but is more restricted. For example, a PAC cannot accept donations from corporations or labor unions, and its individual contributions cannot exceed $5,000 a year. A multicandidate PAC also can contribute only $5,000 per candidate per election, which amounts to $10,000 per candidate in a primary and general election and can give a political party up to $15,000. There are no such limits on a super PAC, but it is not supposed to coordinate directly with candidates; its donors also are supposed to be disclosed to the FEC. But super PACs have found ways to hide the identities of their donors. Corporate billionaires have begun funneling millions into super PACs through shell companies and sham nonprofit groups, which are not required to publicly identify their donors.

Crooked places . . .

This is not government by the people. This is not the will of the people. According to the former Federal Election Commissioner Ann M. Ravel, "at least 87% of Americans—including more than 80% of people in both major parties—favor changes to our campaign laws so that wealth does not dictate political influence."

Once again, the prophet exhorts us to change course: the crooked places made straight. Instead, we took a different path, and the crooked places multiplied.

The years since the *Citizens United* case have seen a major surge in donations by dark-money groups. In 2006, for example, about $5 million in dark-money expenditures flowed into federal campaigns. But in the 2024 presidential campaign alone, super PACs, many of which were financed by dark-money groups, contributed a staggering $1.9 billion. Elon Musk, then the richest person in the world, alone spent $288 million in the election, mostly through a super PAC he created. He would go on to play a key role in the Trump administration as the feckless de facto head of the Department of Government Efficiency (DOGE), eliminating programs that help feed and care for millions of hungry people around the globe, slashing thousands of federal jobs held by ordinary Americans, and showing little regard for or understanding of how these programs have contributed to the true greatness of America.

This is what you get when you have the best politicians that money can buy.

Again I ask, who will protect "the least of these"?

For me, a guy who grew up in public housing, the eleventh of twelve children and the first college graduate in my family, the amount of money spent even to run for public office is mind-blowing. It also poses a moral conundrum. Between the competing campaigns and outside groups, about a half billion dollars was spent on my own 2022 Senate race—the most expensive U.S. Senate race that year and one of the most expensive in history. It's a shame. It's embarrassing. But unfortunately, that's the kind of money it takes to command a seat at the table, to bring the people's voice to the table. I could not unilaterally disarm and win.

And every day, I'm reminded of how high the stakes are. Every day, I see the voices and the needs of ordinary folk being squeezed out of our political system. I saw it in the passage of a budget that cut $900 billion in federal funding from Medicaid, the health insurance program that provides medical coverage for low-income individuals, including pregnant women, children, the elderly, and the disabled. I see it as those in power seek cuts to Head Start and Social Security, which provide for America's youngest and oldest citizens. I see it as the powerful work to grant millions in tax credits to the billionaires who have bankrolled their campaigns.

But I also see the voices of ordinary Americans being shoved to the sidelines in so many other ways. For example, most Americans agree that the prices of prescription drugs are ridiculously high, but the men and women they have elected to represent them in Congress have done precious little about it. Why? The huge influence of the trillion-dollar pharmaceutical industry—Big Pharma—which spends astronomical sums of money advertising their drugs, funneling money to the campaigns of lawmakers, and personally lobbying those same legislators. In 2025, there were 12,674 registered lobbyists, about 23 for every member of Congress, based on data from OpenSecrets, an independent nonprofit organization that tracks and publishes campaign finance and lobbying data.

In 2022, all Democrats voted in favor of passing the Inflation Reduction Act, which included provisions to lower prescription drug costs for people on Medicare and cut federal spending in that area. The measure, signed into law by President Joe Biden, enables the secretary of health and human services to negotiate with drug companies the prices of certain drugs that are covered under Medicare. Imagine that. We had to pass a law to be able to negotiate drug prices. Tell me, what kind of capitalism forbids the buyer of goods (in this case, the American taxpayer) from being able to negotiate the prices of goods the seller wants to sell? Where are the congressional defenders of rugged laissez-faire capitalism when Big Pharma is leveraging its monied influence to make it illegal for Medicare to negotiate a reasonable price for prescription drugs on behalf of its recipients? For years, Big Pharma has enjoyed an enormous return on investment (ROI). That is why it lobbied heavily against the measure, even though the reforms we approved are gradual and modest. To be sure, many lives will be saved by this law, which included my own provision capping the cost of insulin at $35 per month for seniors. I am proud of that work, and I often encounter constituents who tell me about the difference it made for them. Yet the prices of just ten drugs can be negotiated under this law. We took a step in the right direction, but the fight to get there underscored how difficult it is to effect real change, and it left me feeling that increasingly our democracy is owned not by the people but by those with the deepest pockets. Because our electoral system is increasingly awash in money and monied interest, truth be told, both parties are complicit in this sad reality. Campaign finance reform is among the most consequential work we can be doing right now to save our democracy and extend its promise to every citizen.

This will not be easy. Sometimes the magnitude of the challenges facing our democracy feels overwhelming. But it is in those times that I hearken back to Isaiah. When you feel weak, remember, the prophet reminds us there is possibility. There is hope. We can make the rough places smooth.

In his words I find personal solace and direction. It is impossible to separate my role as a pastor from that of public servant. Many times, I have found myself saying exactly those words that Isaiah spoke as he sat in the Temple, awed by the power and grace of the Holy One: If the Lord needs someone, "here am I, send me" (Isaiah 6:8, NIV).

I felt that as I wrestled with my decision to run for the Senate in the first place. When this opportunity emerged, I laid the choice out to my church, calling a kind of town hall meeting one Sunday to discuss it with members of the congregation and Ebenezer's officers. A few hundred people showed up, and it immediately became apparent that not everyone supported the idea of their pastor running for public office. The meeting was tense. Many were nervous. Politics is an ugly game. What would be the implications of their pastor entering the fray during such a fraught and divided time? How would this impact the reputation of the storied Ebenezer Baptist Church? How might politics compromise the pastor's prophetic voice? These were all legitimate and important questions. Yet I knew in my heart that this was the time. Rather than asking if I should run, I instead made an announcement: "Here's what I'm going to do. I would love to have your support."

The first person who spoke was a big, burly member of the church who yelled out defiantly, "It's time for you to go!" Some others agreed. One of my prominent deacons and a life-long member of Ebenezer stood solemnly, noting a run would involve months of campaigning. He suggested the church get an interim pastor. I was stunned and a little hurt. Not even a temporary leave of absence? An interim pastor? Obviously, you would only need an interim pastor if the current pastor were gone, filling a gap until the church could conduct a search and call a new pastor. Honestly, that was a low moment for me. Having faithfully served for fifteen years, I had hoped the people to whom I had dedicated so much of my life would extend enough grace and space to see this through.

Indeed, as I would learn in the meeting, there was a lot of love, even among those who questioned the move, and overwhelming support. One decades-long member, a committed activist, had been a part of the Atlanta student movement and had staged sit-ins and battled racism for many years. Dr. King even presided over her wedding. She was one tough cookie! So when she raised her hand and stood, I got concerned. But she surprised me.

"This is Ebenezer Baptist Church," she said. "It's true that Dr. King never ran for office. But essentially Reverend Warnock is doing what he did. I see no difference. Ebenezer pastors have always taken the ministry beyond the church doors." Another member, who has since also died, warmed my heart when she too, offered, "You've been faithful to us, and to the church. If you feel this is what the Lord wants you to do, I support you." Then came a moment that continues to amaze and move me to this day. Suddenly, one of the deacons burst into an a cappella song: "Guide my feet, Lord, while I run this race," she sang. Others organically joined in singing. "I don't want to run this race in vain." I'd heard the old African American spiritual before, of course, but this time it resonated with a completely different meaning for me, and for us.

Guide my feet while I run this race. I don't want to run this race in vain.

I was undone. I sat there, bent over with my head in my hands, tears streaming. This was a holy moment on holy ground. Only time would tell what the people of Georgia would decide to do. But I had gotten my assignment. My job was to run this race, centering the needs and concerns of the poor, working families, and the middle class, those trying to make a way out of no way. I was so grateful that grace had paved a path for me to do just that amid the tense debates that happen in the public square, to preach the Gospel I had been preaching for years to a larger audience, and in a new way, in a campaign, with all its possibilities and perils. I was in awe. I was afraid. I felt both the blessing and the burden of the moment. History had summoned me. There was no turning back.

Still—and perhaps especially now—there is no turning back. Our democracy is in crisis. Rescuing it will require hard work. Boots on the ground to the polls. Voices crying out, even when it seems they are just echoing in the wilderness. And lots of prayer, the kind backed by action and the expectation fueled by faith.

Our moment of adversity won't last forever.

As we are reminded in Isaiah 30:20–21, "Although the Lord gives you the bread of adversity and the water of affliction, your teachers will be hidden no more; with your own eyes you will see them. Whether you turn to the right or to the left, your ears will hear a voice behind you, saying, 'This is the way; walk in it' " (NIV).

3

TWO THOUSAND VERSES

My then-seven-year-old daughter once turned to me with the most innocent, earnest look of concern and a question: Why do people have to sleep outside? On her regular car rides across Atlanta, including trips to and from our church, the iconic Ebenezer Baptist, she sees homeless men and women sleeping on the streets, and it obviously troubles her sweet, sensitive spirit. I explained that sometimes they're sick and need help. All of us need help, I told her, but some need more than others.

It was my way of saying that the strong must bear the infirmities of the weak and that we must all find ways to show up for one another. It's such a simple concept, but here in the richest country on earth, the gap between the haves and have-nots continues to widen. In 2023, around 37 million Americans (about 11 percent of the population) were living in poverty and struggling to meet their most basic needs. Meanwhile, the number of billionaires in the country has grown from 813 in 2024 to 902 by March 2025. And in 2024, the wealthiest 1 percent of Americans (those with a net worth of at least $13.7 million) controlled 31 percent—nearly a third—of our country's total wealth. That same 1 percent of the wealthiest Americans also owns half of U.S. stocks and mutual funds. Ultimately, the widening gap between the income of a CEO and that of the workers who produce American companies' wealth serves none of us well. American workers do not mind working hard. They just want a fair share of the wealth that they are producing. Instead, because of corporate greed, aided and abetted by legalized bribery in our politics, too many workers endure the contradiction of increasing productivity and decreasing personal wealth. This is unethical and belies any religious claim that seeks to cover it or justify it. Isaiah makes it plain. "Why do we fast, but you do not see? Why humble ourselves, but you do not notice? Look, you serve your own interest on your fast day and oppress all your workers" (Isaiah 58:3, NRSVA). Moreover, this increasing wealth inequality is unsustainable. It is a drag on worker morale and on an American economy fueled largely by the consumerism of everyday people. If America is to secure its future and a thriving economy, those who sit low must be lifted to heights that honor their humanity, while those who occupy lofty places must give some ground to the low.

Our American system of capitalism is based on the hope that anything can happen here, and I certainly don't condemn the genius, hard work, creativity, family legacy, or just plain good fortune that sometimes results in wealth. But as I explained to my daughter when she asked about people sleeping on the streets, we all have a moral obligation to one another, and we share a tied destiny. This calls to mind Isaiah's principle of equity and the promise of a better future for us all. In Isaiah's vision, an equitable society is a place where we can see each other and our shared future more clearly and fully in the preciousness of our humanity. In Isaiah's vision for the land, we all can thrive.

> And if you spend yourselves in behalf of the hungry and satisfy the needs of the oppressed, then your light will rise in the darkness, and your night will become like the noonday. (Isaiah 58:10, NIV)

Equity benefits us all. It was a major preoccupation of the Hebrew prophets, particularly Isaiah. When we help the poor and oppressed, he said, our own dark times will become brighter, "like the noonday." I speak often about poverty because I'm a Matthew 25 kind of Christian. In my life and in my work, I have tried to hear and heed the call of Jesus, who said, "I was hungry, and you gave me food; I was thirsty, and you gave me drink; I was a stranger, and you took me in; I was naked, and you clothed me; I was sick, and you visited me; I was in prison, and you came to me." Some asked the teacher: When were you hungry? When were you thirsty? When were you a stranger, naked, sick, in prison? And Jesus answered, "Truly I tell you, whatever you did for one of the least of these brothers and sisters of mine, you did for me" (Matthew 25:40, NIV). I think often about that passage and so many others. There are some two thousand verses in the Old and New Testaments about the poor and how to treat them. Yet, incredibly, the harshest and meanest voices against poor people in our country are often Christian voices.

It might seem odd that as a pastor, I'm not automatically heartened when I hear that Christians are at the negotiating table. That's because I am, too, a student of history, and I know that in some of this country's crucial moments, Christians have stood on the wrong side of justice. The great abolitionist and freedom fighter Frederick Douglass talked about the hypocrisy of bigoted Christian slave owners in a narrative of his life published in 1845. "Were I to be again reduced to the chains of slavery, next to that enslavement, I should regard being the slave of a religious master the greatest calamity that could befall me," he wrote. "For of all slaveholders with whom I have ever met, religious slaveholders are the worst. I have ever found them the meanest and basest, the most cruel and cowardly, of all others."

More than a century later, Dr. Martin Luther King Jr. wrote in his powerful "Letter from a Birmingham Jail" about the complicity of the white church in the suffering of black people during the cruelest days of the civil rights movement. He reflected on traveling through the South and marveling at its beautiful churches and impressive religious educational buildings. He wrote, "Over and over I have found myself asking: 'What kind of people worship here? Who is their God?'" Where were their voices when segregationist politicians spewed words of hatred and division and enabled violence?

Similarly, when I hear those who call themselves Christians blame poor people for being poor, I wonder, what Bible are they reading? When I consider the unforgiving and punitive policies put forth against poor people, immigrants, refugees, or strangers, as the Bible calls them, I ask, what kind of gospel is this? House Speaker Mike Johnson took a reporter to the Capitol's chapel and mentioned that he had spent much time there, praying as he prepared to lead his fellow U.S. House Republicans in passing the misnomer that is officially named the One Big Beautiful Bill into law. This anything-but-beautiful legislation is robbing millions of poor and working-class Americans of their health care coverage and Supplemental Nutrition Assistance Program (SNAP) benefits while rewarding the wealthiest Americans with yet another large tax cut. The so-called One Big Beautiful Bill passed by Congress and signed by Trump is the most regressive tax bill of my lifetime. It is Robin Hood in reverse! It robs the poor and gives to the wealthy. It is socialism for the rich! In all sincerity, I must ask my Christian brother, what was he praying about? What kind of God would approve of that?

Isaiah has harsh words for a narrow, self-interested piety that ignores the poor. "For day after day they seek me out; they seem eager to know my ways, as if they were a nation that does what is right and has not forsaken the commands of its God," Isaiah says. "They ask me for just decisions and seem eager for God to come near them." Yet, he says, they continue their unrighteous ways, doing the things that please themselves, not God. In the form of a question, Isaiah then lays out what God truly expects, beyond rote religious practices. "Is not this the kind of fasting I have chosen: to loose the chains of injustice and untie the cords of the yoke, to set the oppressed free and break every yoke? Is it not to share your food with the hungry and to provide the poor wanderer with shelter—when you see the naked, to clothe them, and not to turn away from your own flesh and blood?" (Isaiah 58:6–7, NIV)

Isaiah's words are ancient yet still so relevant, speaking to us across the millennia. He could have been talking about the United States. What does it mean to imagine and fight for a world where *every valley shall be exalted and every mountain and hill brought low*? Isaiah repeatedly returns to the topic of inequity and the poor. Equity is a moral mandate. Yet we live in a time and a place where the high sit very high and the low sit very low. The rich are getting richer, and the poor are getting poorer. The poor are also getting sicker.

In 2017, a few years before my election to the U.S. Senate, I gathered with a multifaith coalition to engage in a peaceful protest and prayer session at the United States Capitol, where we were fighting for the right of poor people to have access to health care. I and other clergy were handcuffed and arrested for this altogether peaceful assembly. We expected that. As the arresting Capitol Police officers voiced their instructions, I could hear Isaiah's inspiration and see his vision. An arrest was a small price to pay to push politicians to see poor people's humanity.

Since my election, I have tried to convince Georgia to expand Medicaid and to give around 640,000 people, primarily the working poor, access to the basic health care that's already provided through the Affordable Care Act. Shamefully, Georgia is one of the few states that continue to dig in their heels, refusing to expand Medicaid coverage to the working poor. Not only is this unkind, but it also makes absolutely no sense. It costs the state more money *not* to expand coverage than it would cost us to do it. When the Senate passed the American Rescue Plan of 2021, I fought to include billions of dollars to incentivize holdout states (mostly Southern and red, like my own) to expand Medicaid. I forced the issue, putting my foot down, despite repeated warnings from my colleagues in the Senate that it wouldn't pass. Even some in the Democratic caucus wondered why we should reward holdout states, like Georgia, for stubbornly digging in, while others had done the right thing years earlier without these added incentives I sought to put in a bill. I argued that we were not incentivizing Georgia's bad behavior. We were liberating Georgians who were being held hostage by the bad behavior of a few politicians in a gerrymandered state. That was my position, and I wasn't voting on anything else unless we put this into the bill, I told Senate Majority Leader Chuck Schumer.

Here's what's incredible. The incentives *did* get included in the bill that passed, which meant that holdout states like Georgia had every opportunity to do the right thing. Still, the politicians of my state and others refused to do anything to relieve the suffering of their own people. They did not budge.

On the contrary, they left billions of dollars of incentives on the table and millions of mostly working poor people stranded in the health care coverage gap. Meanwhile, as Georgians subsidize health care in the other forty states that have expanded Medicaid, Georgia hospitals, mostly in rural areas, are closing, and our elderly population, as well as our workforce, is getting sicker and poorer. With billions more now in cuts to Medicaid, the scenario will only get worse.

I can hear the words of Isaiah, echoing in my spirit: "Learn to do good; seek justice, rescue the oppressed, defend the orphan, plead for the widow" (Isaiah 1:17, NRSVUE). Why was equity such a concern for him? While much of contemporary American preaching is narrowly focused on personal piety, we tend to forget that systemic injustice was a central theme for the Hebrew prophets. They were not simply condemning the behavior of a few venal individuals, but rather they were critiquing entire systems that were fundamentally rigged against the poor and marginalized. For Isaiah, as for the other prophets, *mispat*, or equitable justice for all, was a core theme.

These days, struggling families of all creeds and backgrounds rightly discern that something is amiss, and that there is a disconnect between their hard work and their circumstances. They're not wrong. Real wages have been stagnant or in decline for most working people of all races for decades. Amid globalization, deindustrialization, the massive redistribution of wealth upward through tax policies, and other seismic shifts in our world, poor people in the same desperate circumstances have been told that their neighbor is the enemy, when, in fact, they are *all* feeling excluded, overwhelmed, and anxious about their futures.

This matters so much to me because I know firsthand what is possible when Americans decide that their poor are not dispensable. I was number eleven, one of the babies in our blended family of twelve children. We lived in the Kayton Homes public housing complex in Savannah, Georgia, with both hardworking parents—my mother, who stayed home to take care of the family, and my father, an entrepreneur who hauled junk, particularly abandoned cars, and salvaged the metal for cash. It was exhausting work, but my father's income fell short of what was needed to feed and care for our large family. Thanks to the federal food stamp program, my family always had just enough food on the table. I never knew the kind of blinding hunger that can make focusing on school practically impossible. I never had to worry whether I'd be able to eat when I got home. But nearly fourteen million children in the United States in 2023—about one in five of them—were experiencing just that kind of food insecurity, uncertain where or even when they will get their next meal. Yet Trump's big, ugly bill enacted massive cuts to SNAP, and that could result in millions of families with children losing their benefits.

As I grew, my parents enrolled me in Head Start, a program that does for poor children what its name indicates. It gave me a tremendous boost in life by exposing me to preschool reading and literacy and by nurturing my natural curiosity, feeding a child's innate desire to learn. It has done the same for generations of children and also has served as free childcare for their parents. Yet Head Start is among the programs targeted for cuts by the Trump administration. In high school, I was selected for Upward Bound, a Great Society–era program that provides early exposure to higher education for promising students who would be the first in their families to attend college.

The program changed the trajectory of my life by putting me on a college campus for academic and cultural enrichment on weekends and in the summer. College became not just a pipe dream or possibility but the expected next step in my academic journey. Upward Bound is administered and financed by the U.S. Department of Education, but less than two months into his second term, Trump signed an executive order to begin the process of dismantling the department. After a federal judge blocked the administration from following through, it asked the Supreme Court to intervene and put the judge's order on hold. The court has ruled that the administration's proposed deep cuts to gut the education department can resume.

After I graduated from high school, my parents dropped

me off at Morehouse College in Atlanta with a big hug, a lot of love, and Scripture. They didn't have a dime to give me, but with federal-government-financed Pell Grants, low-interest student loans, and, soon enough, a job, I made it through Morehouse. I even went on to earn three additional degrees, including a PhD. The Trump administration has proposed significant cuts to Pell Grants, and this at a time when the cost of college is astronomical. In the 1990s, even after financing my fourth degree, I had amassed a total of just $30,000 in accumulated student loan debt. That would barely be enough today to cover the average cost of college for a single year.

What keeps me awake at night is the recognition that it would be considerably harder for me to achieve what I did as a young person today than it was as a kid growing up in the eighties. Sure, I'd like to think that that seventeen-year-old boy growing up in the Kayton Homes housing projects had inherited enough smarts, grit, stamina, and faith from my parents to make a way out of no way. But the reality is that without the government-subsidized programs that helped to level the playing field for me, the success I have achieved—becoming the first in my family to graduate from college, earning four degrees, attaining the kind of education and life experiences that made it possible for me to become pastor of one of America's great historic churches and get elected to the U.S. Senate—would have been more elusive.

So how can we build a vision of inclusivity where kids who are growing up poor, as I did, whether red, yellow, brown, black, or white, living in inner cities or in Appalachian towns or on native land stolen from their ancestors, know that if they work hard in America, there is a chance for them not only to survive but to thrive? How can we use Isaiah's moral topography to reimagine pathways of possibility for all our children?

Despite the cruelty and messiness of today's politics, I remain hopeful. I still believe that we, the American people, will come to ourselves and turn away from the demagogues of divisiveness, embrace our tied destiny and together build a nation that is more merciful, more just, and ultimately more prosperous for all.

> The poorest of the poor will find pasture, and the needy will lie down in safety. (Isaiah 14:30, NIV)

I often say that we suffer from a poverty not of resources but of moral imagination and from a deficit of courage and vision. As a nation, we should hearken back to the American ingenuity that created the transcontinental railroads and, decades later, the interstate highway system. We have yet to bring to America the high-speed trains that are crisscrossing Asia and Europe. We can create more opportunities in the green-energy space. There's no shortage of wind and sun. How do we harness the technologies that utilize those resources to create a cleaner planet and plenty of new jobs—good middle-class jobs—for Americans? Moreover, how do we advance a bold yet thoughtful whole-of-government approach to addressing both the promises and perils of artificial intelligence (AI) and its revolutionary implications for the job market and every field of human endeavor? And how do we rethink education and create the appropriate training programs so that our young people will be ready for the new economy and no one is left behind?

It is a complete fallacy that poor people don't want to work. They want the dignity of work; they just want to earn a livable wage. I am Jonathan Warnock's son, so I believe strongly in hard work. Throughout my childhood, my father woke me up early every morning the same way: "Get up! Get dressed," he commanded. "Put your shoes on, son! Get ready!" I had to be ready for whatever the day brought, which sometimes meant chores at home, or it could mean helping him work in his junk-hauling business. Occasionally, he would even take me with him on his pastoral rounds to pray for sick and elderly homebound parishioners. But you could not be idle. You had to remain engaged. I guess that's why I don't like seeing young people with nothing to do, nothing they're focused on. We should be creating opportunities for our young people from preschool to college, community college, or vocational training. Let us rise up and build American infrastructure fit for the future and, in so doing, rebuild the American spirit! I think again of Isaiah: "I will turn all my mountains into roads" (Isaiah 49:11, NIV).

As a senator, I've focused on workforce development because I believe that work provides people not just an income but an important sense of purpose. We need to create the kinds of jobs that can help people feel purposeful, proud, alive. The great theologian and fellow Morehouse man Howard Thurman once said, "Don't ask what the world needs. Ask what makes you come alive and go do it. Because what the world needs is people who have come alive."

I met a young man at the DeKalb-Peachtree Airport in Atlanta, and he had the kind of light in his eyes that you want to see in an aspiring professional. He wanted to become a pilot. He had the aptitude and a great attitude, but after ten years he still had not finished his pilot certification training. He was already more than $100,000 in debt, and he had yet to complete the required number of flight hours to be certified as a commercial airline pilot because he could not afford them. But he was working and still determined to finish his training so that he could pursue his passion. His story troubled me deeply because at a time when there is a shortage of aviation workers, including pilots, we have made the path too difficult for young people like this young man, who has everything needed to become a pilot except the resources. When I met him, he was still working toward his goal, but for every young person who refuses to accept a "no" and stays on the journey, how many start out but turn back after, say, four years and $40,000? How many did we lose?

I had that young man in mind when I drafted the AIRWAYS Act, legislation that establishes a grant program to support the education, recruitment, and workforce development of aircraft pilots, aviation maintenance workers, and aviation manufacturing technical workers. It prioritizes the participation of underrepresented populations, including veterans, women, minorities, and individuals in economically disadvantaged geographic areas and rural communities. The legislation also strengthens aviation programs at historically black colleges and universities, community colleges, and technical schools, as well as other institutions of higher learning. I was excited about the possibilities and promise of this legislation when President Biden signed the bill into law in May 2024.

> Every valley shall be exalted, and every mountain and hill brought low. The crooked places shall be made straight, and the rough places smooth. (Isaiah 40:4, NKJV)

When I drafted the AIRWAYS legislation, about 85.4 percent of pilots and flight engineers were white, 2.6 percent were black, and around 6 percent were women. In other words, the aviation industry is largely white and male. That's why I was so disgusted by President Trump's crass, divisive rhetoric after the midair collision between an American Airlines regional jet and a U.S. Army Black Hawk helicopter that killed all sixty-seven people on board and sent both aircraft plunging into the Potomac River near the airport in the Washington, DC, area on January 29, 2025. The morning after the crash, even as rescue teams were still pulling bodies of the deceased from the icy waters, Trump blamed DEI as the cause of the crash. He did so cavalierly, without a scintilla of evidence. When a reporter asked how he could make these claims when investigators were still piecing together the details of the crash, he said, "I have common sense, OK, and unfortunately a lot of people don't. We want brilliant people to do this." He continued, "For some jobs—and not only this but air traffic controllers—they have to be at the highest level of genius." In his wicked way of thinking, keeping the industry white and male is the only way to guarantee "the highest level of genius."

As a country, we need to tap into the genius of *all* Americans. It's not just a moral obligation; it is in our own enlightened self-interest. In a competitive global economy, we don't have time to be divided. I want the twenty-first century, like the twentieth century, to be the American century. I want us as a nation to champion technology, figure out the benefits of artificial intelligence, and use them to advance humanity. We don't want places like China, with its authoritarian regime and communist worldview, to lead the world in artificial intelligence or to set the world order. That would be a different kind of world. So we must embrace a public policy agenda of abundance—an abundance of opportunities for everyone.

It seems right now that we have entered a period akin to the Gilded Age, a time when abundance was limited to the few with unlimited resources, when barons had inordinate wealth and unchecked power. Now, as then, so few have so much and so many have so little.

"Right now, opportunity is not equally distributed in America: People's chances of achieving success vary widely depending upon their parents' income, racial background and zip code," said Harvard economics professor Raj Chetty.

Such is a spiritual and material fraying of the covenant we have with one another in the land of freedom, equality, and opportunity. But we, the people, still have a voice, if we would but use it to protect our democracy. We don't have to sit back and accept the vast wealth inequality gap as simply the price of American capitalism. We can recognize our shared destiny and accept that it is in all our best interests when we channel the collective will and power of the people into public policy and government that do their part to lift "the least of these." We have been able to do just that with good policies, like the expanded child tax credit, which was included in the American Rescue Plan.

In 2021, Congress approved the $1.9 trillion relief package to assist families in their financial recovery from the coronavirus pandemic. We increased the existing child tax credit benefit from $2,000 per child per year to a maximum of $3,600 per child ages six or younger and $3,000 for other children under the age of eighteen. And instead of making families wait to get a lump sum at tax time, we set up the measure so that the funds could be disbursed in monthly payments. Many families received monthly payments of $300 or $250 (depending on the child's age). But what made a huge difference is that we closed a loophole that had left out about one-third of the nation's poor children because their families earned too little to qualify under the income eligibility requirements. Studies showed that most families reported using the funds to help cover their basic needs, including food. And when these families shopped at the local Walmart and grocery stores, the business owners and farmers also benefited. We cut childhood poverty in America by more than 45 percent. Unfortunately, the 2021 expanded benefit expired after just six months because Republicans—the same lawmakers who sanctimoniously describe themselves as pro-life—uniformly bashed the bill as a welfare handout and refused to renew it. That caused the poverty rate to shoot back up, doubling after those six months.

We've seen the good that this kind of policy can do. It was the type of governmental intervention that the Reverend Dr. Martin Luther King Jr. had in mind in 1968 when he planned to lead the Poor People's Campaign, another nonviolent march on Washington, focused this time on economic justice. In his final book, *Where Do We Go from Here: Chaos or Community?*, published the year before, King called for a guaranteed annual income from the government that would help abolish poverty and help poor people live a life of dignity. At the march, his goal was to flood the nation's capital with thousands of poor people who would travel in their old vehicles, even mule carts, and protest income inequality, insufficient wages, and lack of opportunities.

"There is nothing new about poverty. What is new, however, is that we now have the resources to get rid of it," King said in the book. He added, "The time has come for an all-out world war against poverty. . . . The well off and the secure have too often become indifferent and oblivious to the poverty and deprivation in their midst. . . . Ultimately a great nation is a compassionate nation. No individual or nation can be great if it does not have a concern for 'the least of these.'"

King's words are just as relevant today as they were in 1967, when he laid the groundwork for the Poor People's Campaign. King clearly understood that the problem of poverty extends beyond a single community of people, which is why he brought together different racial and ethnic groups to join him in the campaign. But King never made it to that march. He detoured to Memphis to encourage and march with sanitation workers who had gone on strike to protest unequal wages, unsafe working conditions, and inhumane treatment. King saw their issues as connected to those he was taking to Washington with the campaign. But as he stood on the balcony of the Lorraine Motel, where he was staying in Memphis that evening of April 4, 1968, King was shot to death. He literally died trying to help poor people.

I was born a year after Dr. King was assassinated. But as a high school kid, already sensing my call to ministry, I discovered old LP recordings of some of the sermons he had delivered at mass meetings during the civil rights movement, and he became my superhero. He preached a gospel that resonated with me. A gospel that examined the condition of humankind through the Scriptures and called out injustice. Until I found my own voice, I even tried to sound like him. But his spirit—his passion for justice, his love for God and *all* of God's people, and his concern for "the least of these"—lives in me, informing my work and ministry.

I believe that if Dr. King were still with us today, he would be greatly concerned about the lack of access of Americans to affordable housing. The ability to own a home is the cornerstone of the American dream, but the rising cost of rent, high down-payment costs, and a shrinking pool of affordable homes on the market have put that dream out of reach for too many American families today. Infrastructure is spiritual; it honors every child's right to occupy space. I watched my hardworking parents struggle to save with the hope of buying their own home someday. They finally were able to do so much later in life. But I regularly hear from ordinary Americans who worry that they will never own a piece of the dream.

The affordable housing crisis disproportionately impacts young Americans and communities of color. Often, for working-class and poor black and brown parents, their homes were the only things of significant value they could pass on to their children to help build generational wealth. But the high cost of rent is eating up a larger share of incomes, making it nearly impossible to save for a down payment. In 2024, rental costs reached a new high, while the share of first-time homebuyers reached an all-time low. The problem is exacerbated by private equity firms that swoop in, buy up the limited housing stock, and increase housing costs even more.

In their *New York Times* bestseller, *Abundance*, authors Ezra Klein and Derek Thompson say twenty-first-century America is "the story of chosen scarcities." Public policy can make the difference.

"It is not a public policy problem if most households cannot afford a VR headset," Klein and Thompson wrote in their book. "But that cannot be said for housing and education and medicine."

As a member of the Senate Committee on Banking, Housing, and Urban Affairs, I have worked diligently to increase the chances of everyday Americans to own their own homes. I've introduced legislation to spur housing construction, reduce barriers to home ownership (like rent and down-payment assistance), and make it less desirable for private investment firms and corporate investors to buy all the houses on the market. But to make deep and lasting change, we as a nation must prioritize the needs of "the least of these," push our elected leaders to do right by them, and then hold us accountable at the ballot box.

People of faith, particularly, have no excuse to do otherwise. We suffer not from a lack of knowledge. Some two thousand verses in the Scriptures center the poor. Quoting Isaiah, Jesus made clear in his inaugural sermon that he came to "preach good news to the poor." Jesus also corrected those who would marginalize children, chiding his disciples for pushing them away. Too many of the poor people in America and in the world are children. They pay no taxes to our governments, nor do they tithe to our houses of worship. Perhaps that is why children are the casualties of every age.

We who would be disciples of a more excellent way must resist the easy path of discarding the children. Ultimately, it is to our detriment. There are not enough prisons, police, or armies to contain growing numbers of young people who have nothing to lose. Moreover, we lose the incalculable benefits that come with the nurturing and perfecting of their gifts. In this way, whatever our faith tradition or beliefs, we do holy work when we fight so that every child has a chance. What's more, we make the world safer, richer, more prosperous, and more sustainable for our own.

Sometimes, when my two little kids are pestering each other while sitting in the back seat of my car, they ask me to intervene: "Daddy, tell him . . ." Quite often, I just turn around and remind them that they are siblings and are stuck with each other, "so figure it out!" We Americans and citizens of the globe are stuck with one another. So we must figure it out. We are all God's children.

4

SCAR ON THE SOUL OF AMERICA

When I think about the most pressing and consequential domestic issues in American life today, somewhere at the top of my list is mass incarceration. Sure, there are other important issues that confront us, but when you consider the vast tentacles of the carceral state, its impact on every aspect of American life is pervasive.

If you care about poverty, families, and the absence of fathers from their children's lives, you ought to care about mass incarceration, because nothing has siphoned more black men out of our communities than the prison industrial complex. Black bodies have been sucked out of our communities over the last forty years with huge consequences for the women and children they've left behind. If you care about education and children's access to learning, you ought to care about mass incarceration, because our country has spent billions warehousing young people instead of educating them. By all indicators, youths who drop out of school are much more likely to end up behind bars than those who do not, thereby perpetuating the cycle and steadily feeding the insatiable appetite of America's prison industrial complex, the largest in the world. If you care about racism, stereotypes, and stigmas, you ought to care about mass incarceration, because black and brown bodies are disproportionately represented among those behind bars. And the resulting stigma relegates them to second-class citizenship in a permanent caste system that limits their lives and ambitions far beyond their time behind the prison walls.

I was drawn into this work when I realized that the discrimination Dr. King and the civil rights soldiers who marched beside him fought against is reinscribed in the carceral state. Take voting rights, for instance. Many Americans who have paid their debt to society are returned to our society with the expectation that they will be good citizens, but they are denied certain privileges and responsibilities of citizenship. In many states, such as Georgia, they cannot vote or serve on a jury while on probation or parole. They are citizens effectively without citizenship. Moreover, in some states, like Georgia, people who have served time behind bars make up a class of people against whom job discrimination is legal. They might be automatically disqualified from certain jobs that require certifications or licenses. They would not, thus, be able to find even a blue-collar job because they must forever check a box identifying themselves as convicted felons. In some states, they can't qualify for public benefits, such as food stamps. It doesn't matter that they have served their time and paid their debt to society. Some of them haven't even served time; they may have pled guilty to a lesser felony charge just to avoid jail, without fully realizing they would be marked forever by the dreaded *F.* Forever marked as former felons, returning citizens will experience more difficulty finding work and housing, the most basic components of adult life. Is it any wonder this nation's recidivism rate is so high, as most returning citizens land back behind bars within just three to five years of their initial arrest?

The Bible tells us in Micah 6:8 that God requires His people "to act justly and to love mercy" (NIV). But our criminal justice system can be the polar opposite: brutal, unforgiving, sometimes even vicious.

The United States, a democracy of 340 million people, has both a greater number and a greater percentage of its people incarcerated than any other large nation in the world. Not even China, a dictatorship with a population of 1.4 billion people, comes close. Neither do any of the other repressive nations whose human rights records we Americans deplore. North Korea. Iran. Russia. This nation makes up less than 5 percent of the world's population, yet it houses more than 20 percent of the world's prisoners. And a disproportionate share of those incarcerated in our country are black, making up 41 percent of the prison and jail populations but only 14 percent of U.S. residents, according to a 2025 report by the Prison Policy Initiative. But what I find most troubling is that for all the herding away and human warehousing we've done, mass incarceration has not made us any safer.

We as a society have chosen to invest in incarceration instead of investing in the kinds of community-based programs that would help tackle some of the larger social issues at the root of the problem. Criminal justice scholar James Forman Jr. argues for a reimagined system of criminal justice that prioritizes community safety *and* well-being and provides alternatives that focus on rehabilitation and restoration—mental health counseling, job training, housing assistance, and more. He says individuals can play a role by supporting such programs, serving on juries, and voting for progressive prosecutors who believe in reform. Reimagining our criminal justice system will require courage among lawmakers and others who have the power to change things, steadfast advocacy, and hearts determined to do what is right.

"Mass incarceration was built bit by bit, law by law, choice by choice, over generations, across our fifty states, Washington, DC, the territories, and over three thousand counties. It will have to be dismantled the same way," Forman and fellow editors Premal Dharia and Maria Hawilo wrote in the introduction to their 2024 book, *Dismantling Mass Incarceration: A Handbook for Change.*

I'm reminded of the time in our history when a few faithful denizens of these lands rose with courage and compassion against the brutal institution of slavery. As early as 1688, four brave Quakers from Germantown (now part of Philadelphia) organized the first religious protest against slavery in Britain's American colonies there. They based their call for the abolition of slavery on the Christian biblical principle, commonly known as the Golden Rule, "Do to others as you would have them do to you" (Matthew 7:12, NIV).

By the way, there are iterations of the Golden Rule in practically all of the great faith traditions and other moral traditions. Judaism says, "That which is hateful to you, do not do to your fellow. That is the whole Torah; the rest is commentary" (Talmud, Shabbat 31a). Islam avers, "None of you truly believes until he loves for his brother that which he loves for himself" (Hadith). Hinduism asserts, "This is the sum of duty: Do not do to others what would cause you pain if done to you" (Mahabharata). Buddhism echoes the same teaching: "Hurt not others in ways that you yourself would find hurtful" (Udanavarga). Confucianism counsels, "Do not do to others what you do not want them to do to you" (Analects). Yet the Baha'i faith puts the same universal teaching in an active and positive rather than negative frame. It says, "Choose thou for thy neighbor that which thou choosest for thyself" (Tablets of Baha'u'llah). I like that framing because it suggests that not only are we commanded to do our neighbor no harm, but we are, in fact, summoned to seek our neighbor's welfare and well-being. Choose for your neighbor what you would choose for yourself! Fight for your neighbor the way you would fight for yourself! Not only in a spiritual sense but in a material and practical sense, you are indeed fighting for yourself!

The Quakers caught the spirit of that, and so at a time when many of their fellows were enslavers, they took an active stand against slavery. Though the denomination would wrestle internally over the issue for nearly a century, in 1776 the Quakers would become the first large white Christian denomination in America to forbid members to enslave people. Many Quakers also would play a crucial role in the Underground Railroad, providing safe spaces for the enslaved who were fleeing to freedom up north.

I think of William Lloyd Garrison, the uncompromising abolitionist and newspaper publisher who advocated vehemently for the immediate end to slavery and refused to abide any other position or anyone who believed otherwise. "I do not know how to worship God and Mammon at the same time," he said in an 1854 speech decrying slavery. "If other men choose to go upon all fours, I choose to stand erect, as God designed every man to stand. If, practically falsifying its heaven-attested principles, this nation denounces me for refusing to imitate its example, then, adhering all the more tenaciously to those principles, I will not cease to rebuke it for its guilty inconsistency."

The great orator Frederick Douglass, who escaped slavery and became the most influential black abolitionist, was also a licensed preacher. But he denounced the Christianity practiced by white Americans for their hypocrisy on the issue of slavery. "I love the pure, peaceable, and impartial Christianity of Christ: I therefore hate the corrupt, slaveholding, women-whipping, cradle-plundering, partial and hypocritical Christianity of this land," he explained in an appendix to later editions of his 1845 autobiography. "Indeed, I can see no reason, but the most deceitful one, for calling the religion of this land Christianity. I look upon it as the climax of all misnomers, the boldest of all frauds, and the grossest of all libels."

Just a small contingent of Christians got the Gospel right and joined the abolitionist movement back then. Most Christian churches, particularly throughout the South, were proslavery, even using the Bible to justify their racist ideology and practices. And too many others witnessed the degradation of humans, treated as chattel, and didn't say a word. Today many of us look back at those generations and wonder how so many people, especially people of faith, stayed silent. Likewise, I believe future generations someday will turn the questions on us: Where did we stand, what did we say, and what did we do as the land of the free became the mass-incarceration capital of the world? Someday we must answer to the God of love and justice.

In that spirit, I approached the Reverend Dr. Katharine Rhodes Henderson, then-president of Auburn Theological Seminary in New York, in 2017 with the idea of bringing faith leaders together to work on criminal justice reform. I was at the time a senior fellow at Auburn, a two-hundred-year-old seminary that is also a leadership institute that trains faith leaders for social justice activism in the public square. As senior pastor at Ebenezer, I proposed a partnership between Auburn and Ebenezer to launch a faith-based response to mass incarceration. Together, Dr. Henderson and I invited the Temple, Atlanta's oldest and most prominent Reform Jewish congregation, led by Rabbi Peter Berg, to join us in convening what would become the Ending Mass Incarceration campaign. I knew then, as I know now, that the only way to move forward was through the work of intentional inclusivity—of all faith traditions, of all racial backgrounds, and of all political persuasions. The call went out to faith leaders with this urgent message: The judgment of God is upon us. We are summoned to this moral moment to address this deep and abiding contradiction to the covenant we have with one another. Mass incarceration is a scar on the soul of our country.

More than four hundred people answered the call in June 2019, showing up for the plenary and breakout sessions of the two-day conference in Atlanta to end mass incarceration; an additional one thousand people came for the opening session. We were Christians, Jews, Muslims. We were young, old, formerly incarcerated, public policy workers, parents, all passionate and purposeful about learning, sharing ideas, and walking away with an action plan for our faith communities to make an impact. With a nod to the biblical story of Moses and his God-led confrontation of Pharaoh before leading the Israelites out of Egypt, we named our conference "Let My People Go: Ending Mass Incarceration."

> Then the Lord said to Moses, "Go to Pharaoh and say to him, 'Thus says the Lord: Let my people go, so that they may worship me.'" (Exodus 8:1, NRSV)

As I saw it, just as Moses was called to liberate those in Egyptian bondage so that they might worship—that is, live lives of faithful and productive human thriving under the aegis of the One in whose image we are created—we people of faith are called to speak for the incarcerated in a nation that too often criminalizes the poor, that warehouses them and renders them invisible. There's something utterly inhumane about being rendered invisible. As awful as slavery was, at least the enslaved were visible. I've talked to many mothers of people who are incarcerated, black, brown, and white, and they feel forgotten, that their children are forgotten. It's hard for people to advocate for those they don't even see.

Many of the faith leaders who attended the conference have continued doing the work as the Multifaith Initiative to End Mass Incarceration. By scaling up our networks locally and statewide, we continue to grow and expand. Our June 2024 conference took place in Dallas, Texas, exemplifying the kind of ongoing work we are committed to as individuals and as a collective. We train churches to launch cash bail-relief campaigns in their cities and organize record-expungement events, all the while challenging the contradictions in our criminal justice system. Our aim is in keeping with Isaiah's vision of equity, inclusivity, integrity, and possibility. Our daily work is to continue to create a future that honors the capacity for restoration, rehabilitation, and redemption inherent in us all. Ebenezer, too, has maintained the work, collaborating with celebrities and other groups to provide bail relief for the poor. Many of the men and women sitting behind bars are there simply because they cannot afford to pay their bail. Being able to pay bail doesn't mean you're less dangerous. Being unable to pay does not mean you're more dangerous. The opposite is just as likely to be true. But our criminal justice system has made being poor a crime.

This is exemplified in the Ferguson Report, which details the findings of the U.S. Justice Department's Civil Rights Division's investigation into the police department in Ferguson, Missouri, after the fatal shooting of Michael Brown, an unarmed eighteen-year-old, by a white police officer in 2014. The shooting unleashed the black community's simmering rage in protests that captured the national spotlight. While a grand jury and a federal investigation each cleared the white officer of criminal wrongdoing, the Department of Justice report on Ferguson's police department and municipal courts revealed disturbing patterns of racial stereotyping and discrimination, as well as pervasive corruption. The investigators found that the police department was more motivated by raising revenue than by responding to the community's public safety needs, often resulting in aggressive tactics that violated the residents' constitutional rights. The city and its criminal justice system functioned financially on the backs of poor people, most of whom were black. For example, city officials annually budgeted large revenue increases based on municipal fines and fees and then pushed the police department and court to deliver with more traffic tickets and fines to cover the increased expenses. For a person struggling to make ends meet, an inability to pay the fine for a minor traffic infraction and a missed court appearance could easily spiral into disaster. "Minor offenses can generate crippling debts, result in jail time because of an inability to pay, and result in the loss of a driver's license, employment, or housing," the report said.

Such crooked places.

I can't help but think of Kalief Browder, the young black man arrested in 2010 in New York City at age sixteen and accused of stealing a backpack. The backpack was not found on him, he refused to take a plea deal, and he vigorously proclaimed his innocence. Yet he remained locked up at the notorious Rikers Island jail complex for three years while waiting for his day in court. Three years! He spent an equivalent of two of those years in solitary confinement and was beaten by prison guards multiple times. The experience so traumatized him that he tried to end his life while in prison. Eventually, the bogus charges were dropped, and Browder was released. As his case drew attention from the media, celebrities, and politicians, Browder tried mightily to recapture his life. But the damage to his soul was deep. Browder died by suicide on June 6, 2015. Having been released from a dank prison cell and the trauma of solitary confinement, the dark shadows yet stalked him until he succumbed unto death. The system killed him; he did not kill himself. His mother had become an advocate for prison reform, but, surely heartbroken by his death, she suffered a fatal heart attack a year later. Two souls claimed by the injustice of our criminal *justice* system, one that is sometimes more criminal than just.

Bryan Stevenson, executive director of the Equal Justice Initiative, has said that in America's criminal justice system, it is better to be rich and guilty than to be poor and innocent. Stevenson, a highly acclaimed lawyer, has dedicated his life to helping the poor and incarcerated, particularly those condemned to die in prison. He and his team have helped to free or obtain sentencing relief for more than 140 people who were wrongly convicted and sentenced to death, as well as for many others who were wrongly convicted or unfairly sentenced. Stevenson has won many other significant legal challenges, including a 2019 U.S. Supreme Court ruling that protects prisoners who suffer from dementia from execution. His successes also include a groundbreaking 2012 Supreme Court ruling that banned sentences of mandatory life imprisonment without parole for juvenile offenders, ages seventeen and under. So Stevenson, perhaps better than anyone, knows well the outsize role that wealth and race play in determining who gets locked up and who doesn't. Too often, they are *the* determining factors. Given these truths, we desperately need some integrity in our land. Isaiah rebukes those "who acquit the guilty for a bribe and deprive the innocent of their rights" (Isaiah 5:23, NRSVA). Are we willing to look honestly at our broken criminal justice system? Are we willing to see how it raises deep questions about our integrity?

For years, I have argued that at the root of America's highly racialized carceral state is a spiritual problem. When Dr. King and others formed the Southern Christian Leadership Conference at Ebenezer in 1957 to expand the civil rights movement, their goal and their motto captured the essence of the work that lay ahead, work that would reach far beyond the sit-ins and marches, work that would "redeem the soul of America." Then, as now, America has a soul problem. Decades of mass incarceration have added yet another deep scar on the soul of America.

Author Michelle Alexander, a civil rights attorney and brilliant legal scholar, was a keynote speaker at the 2019 mass-incarceration conference for faith leaders. In her powerful 2010 book, *The New Jim Crow: Mass Incarceration in the Age of Colorblindness*, she makes the persuasive argument that mass incarceration is America's new system of subjugating black people. I agree 100 percent. In terms of domestic issues, mass incarceration may be the central moral issue of our time. The mass incarceration rate, particularly that of black people, is so much worse than Dr. King could have imagined when he was leading marches for racial justice throughout the South. From the mid-1960s through the 2000s, the incarceration rate increased by 600 percentage points, according to Alexander in a 2014 PBS interview and in the revised edition of her book.

"More African American adults are under correctional control today—in prison or jail, on probation or parole—than were enslaved in 1850, a decade before the Civil War began," Alexander reported in her book. Her analysis was based on the estimated 2.4 million black adults who were under correctional supervision in 2007, compared with the 1.7 million ages fifteen and older who were enslaved in 1850. While there has been some improvement, nearly 2 million black people remain under correctional supervision in jails, in prisons, and on probation and parole, based on mass-incarceration numbers provided by the nonprofit, nonpartisan think tank Prison Policy Initiative.

This troubling condition did not happen by accident. It was due in large part to the country's so-called war on drugs, first declared by President Richard Nixon in the 1970s and heightened by successive presidents with more punitive drug laws and harsher penalties. President Ronald Reagan declared his war on drugs in 1982, and contrary to popular opinion, crack didn't emerge as a crisis in black urban neighborhoods until three years later, Alexander points out. But the Reagan administration saw an opportunity to generate support for his war and even hired staff to mount a public awareness campaign about the growing crack epidemic. Suddenly, sensationalist news stories and images were everywhere, telling of crack dealers and gang wars, emaciated mothers selling their bodies for a high and babies born addicted and abandoned. Almost all their faces were black. Lawmakers opined about the drug's highly addictive nature and passed laws that established significantly harsher penalties for crimes associated with crack. Those harsh penalties set crack apart from cocaine, which was essentially the same drug in a different form but was mostly associated then with white people and wealth. Money flowed into law enforcement agencies to fight the war. At the same time, the post–World War II industrial boom began to fade, taking steady, well-paying jobs from residents of inner cities across the nation. The incarceration rate exploded, and America began investing in an expansive prison industrial complex that soon included private, for-profit penal institutions and associated businesses, all feeding off the desperation of the poor.

At a time when we as a nation could have shifted to preparing our young people for postindustrial America and moving to an information technology–based society, deploying our resources to get kids ready for the next generation of work, we instead invested in the drug war. By the way, studies show that black people and white people use and sell drugs at roughly the same rates. The difference is in the location, manner, patterns, and practices of policing and prosecution. No one does "stop and frisk" in corporate suites or in the dormitories of colleges and universities. That happens in the valleys, the low places. Those valleys that Isaiah spoke about are exploited rather than exalted. We built a prison industrial complex, warehousing more bodies than any nation in the world. In another tragic episode of our nation's history, we once again made black and brown bodies the product, on the market, for profit.

There are many unclean hands.

Ironically, America's so-called war on drugs and its massive prison industrial complex—the intermingling of public and private sectors that profit from those behind bars and their loved ones—bespeaks its own kind of addiction: an addiction to the revenue that props up entire towns, the profits that enrich the bail-bond industry and dozens of other industries from telecommunications to snacks, medicine, and construction. Weaning ourselves off these for-profit industries that benefit from mass incarceration would require the kind of moral courage and integrity that inspired the abolitionist movement more than a century and a half ago. The question is, do we have the courage and the moral imagination necessary to divest from the politics and machinery of fear, death, and life sentences for nonviolent drug-related offenses? Do we have the courage and moral imagination to invest in life-giving programs for all our children? Like the expanded child tax credit, which had briefly cut child poverty in this country by half.

Can we imagine a different reality, one of Isaiah's prophetic possibilities? In this context, where the "low" are made "high," those with mental disabilities or trauma, for example, would not be left to fend for themselves in a system that is intrinsically pitted against them. But rather, a new possibility would hold that those same legal structures and institutions should actively work toward the ultimate uplift of all citizens, no matter how desperate or meager their circumstances. A new possibility would have as its central tenet the understanding that the uplift of each one of us ultimately lifts us all, together. "Choose for your neighbor what you would choose for yourself."

During my last year or two at Morehouse College, I heard a statistic that stopped me: More black men were in jail, in prison, or on probation or parole than in colleges and universities. That reality hit me hard. There I was, a poor kid from humble beginnings, by the grace of God and the goodness of so many, able to make my way through Morehouse, a bastion of upstanding black manhood, leadership, and service, on the way to pursuing my dreams. Meanwhile, so many young black men who looked like me and were about my age were ensnared in a judicial system that cared little about their futures. That was the humbling moment when I began paying closer attention to matters of racial justice and incarceration.

After graduating from Morehouse, I pursued my master's and doctorate degrees at Union Theological Seminary in New York and worked at the historic Abyssinian Baptist Church in Harlem, first as an intern minister, then as the youth minister, and then as the assistant pastor. Abyssinian has always been the kind of place where people from the pulpit to the pews walk out their faith, often challenging the status quo. Under the leadership of the Reverend Dr. Calvin O. Butts III, the social gospel was preached there regularly—the kind Dr. King preached, the kind where biblical teachings extend beyond personal salvation to our responsibility as Christians to impact the world and the people in it. Reverend Butts sometimes preached about the growing numbers of our black brothers and sisters being incarcerated. He even talked about planning a march to Rikers Island. Though that march never happened, the message left an impression on me. But nothing made the issue of mass incarceration more real to me than when my older brother, Keith, got arrested in 1997.

Keith is five years older than I and next in line in our

blended family of twelve siblings. My father was divorced with a son and three daughters when he met my mom, who also was divorced, with five sons and a daughter. After they married, I was born, followed by my younger sister, making the kids an even dozen. Keith would serve in the U.S. Army and then join the police force in our hometown. He had worked as an officer for less than two years when he was implicated in an FBI undercover operation that netted the arrests of eleven officers, all black, accused of colluding with drug dealers. My brother was charged with aiding and abetting the distribution of cocaine by providing security for the dealers.

Our entire family was shocked. My parents, both Pentecostal preachers, had raised us all in the church and maintained a strict but loving home full of family fun and laughter. I was disappointed in my brother, angry, and concerned about his future. As part of the drug war, lawmakers had imposed harsh mandatory-minimum sentences for drug crimes. Sure enough, I would watch helplessly as the system made a punitive example of my brother. Keith, then thirty-three, was found guilty and sentenced to life in prison without the possibility of parole. In the federal system, a life sentence means just that, a lifetime behind bars. It was a devastating, jaw-dropping sentence for a nonviolent crime committed by a military veteran with no prior criminal history. My brother had made a terrible mistake. I didn't understand it, nor did I condone or excuse it.

But this I knew: His life was still valuable. He was not disposable or unworthy of redemption. So as his little brother and as a pastor who believes in mercy and redemption, I vowed to fight for Keith with everything in me.

It was a Goliath-sized battle for twenty-two years. Twenty. Two. Years. We exhausted every possible argument and appeal. On the inside, Keith did his part, staying out of trouble and maintaining model behavior while staying relatively safe and alive, which itself was no small feat while in federal prison. Ultimately, a worldwide pandemic—a giant itself—brought down the giant we were facing. As the deadly coronavirus began sweeping through communities across the country, eventually taking more than a million lives, President Trump signed into law the Coronavirus Aid, Relief, and Economic Security (CARES) Act, which had been passed by Congress to provide emergency economic relief to families and businesses, hit hard financially after the world shut down to wait out the pandemic. To avoid a further and more deadly spread of the virus in federal prisons, the measure also expanded the home-confinement program, enabling incarcerated individuals who had committed nonviolent crimes, were medically vulnerable, and met other criteria to be released from prison to serve their sentences under home confinement. My brother, fifty-five years old by then, was among those who were released in the summer of 2020. He moved in with our elderly mother, became her primary caretaker, got a job, and was monitored by prison officials around the clock. He was allowed to leave home only to go to work and occasionally attend church. But it was a joyous reunion of our family.

Though the pandemic forced lawmakers and prison officials to look at incarceration differently, the home-confinement program showed what is possible if we as a nation are serious about addressing mass incarceration. The program enabled prison officials to reduce the prison population quickly at a significant savings to taxpayers without compromising public safety. And it has been a resounding success. According to a report written in 2023 by my friend and colleague U.S. Senator Cory Booker, 13,204 individuals were placed in home confinement under the authority of the CARES Act. Of those, just twenty-two people were rearrested for a new offense, and most of those arrests were for drugs or minor crimes. That is a recidivism rate of less than 0.2 percent.

Our system at times has made small steps in the right direction. For example, during his first term in December 2018, President Trump signed the First Step Act, a bipartisan criminal justice reform bill passed by Congress, the result of many years of lobbying by advocates. As I said at the time in an editorial I wrote for *The Atlanta Journal-Constitution*, I rarely ever agree with President Trump or his administration, but I supported this legislation because it made important changes to our justice system. For example, the law reduces some mandatory-minimum sentences and enables men and women in federal prisons to reduce their sentences by participating in programs that have been proven to reduce recidivism and provide the kind of life skills needed for successful reentry into society. The law also gives judges more discretion in issuing sentences lower than the mandatory minimum in sentencing low-level, nonviolent drug offenders.

One of the provisions that I found especially significant is that the 2018 law furthered the work of the Obama-era Fair Sentencing Act, which greatly reduced the disparities between crack cocaine and powder cocaine offenses but was not retroactive. Under the First Step Act, those who received such unfair sentences prior to the bill's passage became eligible to petition for retroactive relief. This alone offered the real hope of sentence reductions and real relief for thousands of people serving time in federal prisons under those unfair sentences, most of them people of color. This law demonstrates what lawmakers can do when we put aside our political differences and work together for the common good. This is the kind of collaboration that will be needed on this issue, moving forward. This is the kind of work that actually makes our communities safer.

What is not needed is the kind of petty politics that threatened to send the folks who were succeeding in home confinement under the CARES Act back to jail. Most who were released from prison early under the CARES Act completed their sentences at home. But by late May 2023, a total of 3,627 people remained in the program, and there was justifiable fear among them that they would have to return to prison. As Trump's first presidential term was winding down in January 2021, his Office of Legal Counsel issued a memo saying that this category of people would be required to return to prison once an end to the Covid-19 emergency was declared. It didn't matter that they had reintegrated into society and become productive citizens, working, helping their families, and contributing to our economy. So advocates got to work, lobbying President Biden when he took office. His Office of Legal Counsel reversed that recommendation, but many of us who supported the home-confinement program were concerned that this population would remain vulnerable to the whims of vindictive politicians. Then, in October 2023, some of my Republican colleagues began circulating proposed legislation that would return those who had been released on home confinement under the CARES Act to prison. We needed a more permanent solution, but the nation was about to be thrust into one of the most consequential presidential campaigns in recent history.

Momentum was building among conservatives for a second Trump presidency, which Democrats worried would be more destructive to our democracy, given the ultraconservative Project 2025 agenda that was floating around, threatening to undermine the progress we had made thus far. On July 21, 2024, President Biden, realizing that he was losing vital support in our party, announced his withdrawal from the presidential race and endorsed Vice President Harris as the Democratic candidate. About a week later, he invited me, along with several other lawmakers and civil rights leaders, to journey with him on Air Force One to the LBJ Presidential Library in Austin, Texas, where he was set to deliver the keynote address commemorating the sixtieth anniversary of the Civil Rights Act. Later the same day, we—now including Lynda Bird Johnson Robb, the eldest daughter of former President Lyndon B. Johnson—would travel to Houston to pay our respects to Congresswoman Sheila Jackson Lee, who had died and was lying in state at Houston's city hall.

Shortly after takeoff, I asked a member of President Biden's staff if I could have a few private moments with him before the day was over. It was a long day, packed with emotion. But at about 10:30 p.m., as we were heading back to Washington, the staffer came to me and said the president would see me. As I entered, President Biden was sitting at his desk working. He said, "Come on in, Rev!"

I thanked him for seeing me and told him I was proud of working with him all these years. He surely didn't need my accolades, but I wanted him to know that I thought he had been an extraordinary president whose legislative achievements and broadly diverse confirmations to the judiciary and other areas of government had pushed us closer to a more racially just and equal society. But there was more he could do. I told him that he had an opportunity to use his clemency power as president to have a tremendous impact on three groups of people deserving of consideration. I talked about the unfairness and racial bias in the application of the death penalty in this country and shared that most of the men on death row in the federal system were sentenced during a different era. I talked about the next group of people who had received far more excessive sentences due to the disparities in crack and cocaine penalties, people whose sentences already would have been completed if they had been sentenced more justly. And I talked about the third group, people who had been released to home confinement under the CARES Act. I unfolded a piece of paper and handed it to him. "Mr. President, this is the work I've done for you," I said, handing him the sheet full of statistics and relevant data. "I know something about this CARES group because one of them is my brother."

He looked at me compassionately, and I shared that my brother was illustrative of what this opportunity meant. He had served by then nearly twenty-six years (the last four under home confinement) and had been a model prisoner, taking advantage of every opportunity to improve himself, working every day, contributing to society. I told President Biden that after doing everything the system required, this group faced the real possibility of having to return to prison. "It would be a miscarriage of justice, sir, for him and people like him to live the rest of their lives under social control," I said.

He told me that he would seriously consider them, and I thanked him for his time.

By the end of the year, President Biden had announced that he was commuting the sentences of thirty-seven of the forty people on federal death row to life without the possibility of parole; the other three had been convicted of hate crimes or terrorism. And he commuted the sentences of the nonviolent drug offenders and those serving time at home under the CARES Act to time served. One of them was my own brother. He has since gotten married and purchased his own home. President Biden, a man of strong faith, kept his word.

Twenty-six years was a long time, and I got discouraged at times along the way; we all do. But when we get tired of the work of bending the moral arc, remember that God's vision for the land in Isaiah is a vision of equity, of inclusivity, of justice for all.

> Every valley shall be exalted, and every mountain and hill brought low. The crooked places shall be made straight, and the rough places smooth.
> (Isaiah 40:4, NKJV)

5

GUNS EVERYWHERE

On May 3, 2023, I got word that an active shooter had opened fire inside a medical facility in Midtown Atlanta. Five people had been shot, one fatally. Nearby schools were on lockdown, including those of my own two elementary school–aged children. The situation was still developing. I felt such sorrow for the victims, who were gunned down in a place where they expected to be safe, a place where people had gone for healing. Those were a scary few hours for me as a parent.

Since I was working in Washington that day, I took to the Senate floor to speak directly about what was unfolding back home in my backyard and our responsibility to do something.

I urged my Senate colleagues to step up and do more about gun violence, but first I bemoaned the loss of our sense of safety in this country:

> It is not right for us to live in a nation where nobody is safe, no matter where they are. We're not safe in our schools. We're not safe in our workplaces. We're not safe at the grocery store. We're not safe at movie theaters. We're not safe at spas. We're not safe in our houses of worship. There is no sanctuary in the sanctuary.

I had been in the Senate then just over two years, and already this was my second time addressing my colleagues after a mass shooting in my home state. I told them I was proud that in the previous congressional session, we had passed the first significant gun-safety legislation in nearly three decades, the Bipartisan Safer Communities Act, which President Biden signed into law on June 25, 2022. The law expanded background checks on people under the age of twenty-one who are seeking to buy a gun. It added boyfriends to an existing law that prohibited people convicted of domestic abuse from buying or owning a gun for five years, and it created financial incentives for states to implement "red flag laws" that allow firearms to be removed temporarily from individuals deemed a threat to themselves or others. The measure had been a long time coming.

Before 2022, the last major gun-safety laws were the Brady Handgun Violence Prevention Act of 1993, mandating federal background checks for firearm purchases through licensed dealers and a five-day waiting period for handgun purchases. The Federal Assault Weapons Ban, signed into law by President Bill Clinton the next year, implemented a ten-year ban on the manufacture of certain semiautomatic assault weapons for civilians. Both were important steps in the right direction, but then progress stalled. When the Assault Weapons Ban expired in 2004, attempts to renew it failed, which was a giant step backward. In the intervening nearly thirty years after the law first passed, so many lives were cut short by gun violence of all kinds. And the mass murders at schools continued.

Even after the massacre at Columbine High School in 1999, when twelve students and a teacher were shot to death and twenty-one others were injured by two teenage gunmen, ages seventeen and eighteen—Congress hosted some fiery speeches and heated debates but ultimately did nothing. I was a graduate student in theology at the time, and I remember the shock and horror of witnessing the awful carnage in the live television coverage in the aftermath of the shooting. The deadliest mass school shooting at the time, it dominated the news coverage for days. We had never seen anything like it.

What we could not have known was that this was the opening chapter of a strange, new American exceptionalism. Unlike any other nation that is not at war, we Americans have accommodated our collective conscience to a tragic ritual of watching the massacre of schoolchildren in random places, year after year, decade after decade. Sadly, it is so well rehearsed that we all have the liturgy of the bloody, sacrificial ritual down pat: witness with horror; mourn the loss; express outrage; tell the stories of the victims; offer thoughts and prayers; argue about why this is happening; move on with our lives. Wash, rinse, repeat. But our hands are still bloody. Any nation that tolerates this kind of killing, offering "thoughts and prayers" while refusing to do what it can to save its own children, has bloody hands. Again, it calls to mind words from Isaiah, who said, "Even though you make many prayers, I will not listen; your hands are full of blood" (Isaiah 1:15, NRSV). We have hidden behind our rhetoric and public rituals, normalizing that which is clearly not normal or necessary. Yet a whole generation of American young adults, some now in their thirties, know nothing else. The tragic ritual at the altar of a nation that has turned guns into idols and violence into a sad and sick kind of worship continues.

Even after Virginia Tech, after Sandy Hook, after Parkland, Congress did nothing.

Then, on May 24, 2022, an eighteen-year-old gunman entered Robb Elementary School in Uvalde, Texas, with an AR-15-style rifle and took the lives of nineteen students, all nine-, ten-, and eleven-year-olds, and two teachers as they hid inside their classrooms. The shooter also injured another seventeen people. Just ten days earlier, the news media everywhere had flashed stories about a mass shooting in Buffalo, New York, where an eighteen-year-old white supremacist shot to death ten black people at a supermarket and injured three more. Finally, about a month after those shootings, a new Congress, with Democrats back in control of both the House and the Senate for the first time in ten years, passed the Bipartisan Safer Communities Act.

I have no doubt the law is saving lives, but it was modest reform. Yet even that was apparently too much to ask, as the second Trump administration, at the behest of the gun lobby, set out to freeze and rescind the funds appropriated for mental health care and other programs provided for in that bipartisan law. The Republican members who voted for the law, even those who had publicly championed it, said nothing and offered no defense for its continuation when asked. As we have done time and time again, we as a nation took one step forward and two steps back on gun safety.

And so there I was again in September 2024, on a rainy night in rural Georgia, mourning schoolchildren who had died in yet another mass shooting at their school. This time, four people—two teachers and two students—were killed and nine others were injured at Apalachee High School in Winder,

Georgia. I gathered for a vigil with families, parents, and community members, all traumatized by the shooting. As I sat outside on an open field on a Friday night with students, parents, teachers, coaches, and friends, it brought me back to my old days playing in the Johnson High School marching band, as it occurred to me that we should all be there for a high school football game—not this. I thought, "What in God's name are we doing to our children?!" I was there to offer comfort even while my own heart ached. I told them I grieved with them as a parent who understood what it was like to drop off your children at school with the expectation that you would pick them up a few hours later. "But increasingly in the United States of America, we can't take for granted that we will pick our children up," I told them. "This is every parent's nightmare."

I extended my prayers, but even as we pray, I explained, we can't just pray with our lips; we must pray with our legs by taking action. "This is not, for me, a political issue," I said. "It is a moral issue. I do not believe that mass shootings as routine are the cost of freedom. I believe it is the cost of blind obstinance. God give us courage. We do not have to live this way."

I left them with the words of Scripture: "The light shines in the darkness, and the darkness overcomes it not" (John 1:5, NRSV).

After the vigil, I met in a private room with family members of the victims. The father of Christian Angulo, a fourteen-year-old student who died in the shooting, shared with me the tragic irony that his family had moved from California to this small town in Georgia to find a quiet, peaceful life.

There is no sanctuary in the sanctuary.

We as a nation can and must do better. Mass shootings—incidents in which at least four people are injured or killed by a firearm—occur every day in the United States, often multiple times a day. In 2024, there were 503 mass shootings, including 30 incidents of mass murder (at least four victims, not including the shooter), according to the Gun Violence Archive, a nonprofit organization that compiles such statistics in an online database. Again, there is no other country in the world where this routinely happens when there is no war. This is American exceptionalism at its worst, and it impacts us all. Even if you do not know anyone who is a victim or survivor of a mass shooting, we are ever reminded that that can change at any moment. As Dr. King once said, "We are caught in an inescapable network of mutuality, tied in a single garment of destiny. Whatever affects one directly, affects all indirectly."

I am ever grateful to God that my children made it home safely after several excruciating hours following the shooting at the medical facility in Atlanta that day. When they arrived, I asked my six-year-old daughter on FaceTime if she understood what had happened at school. Her answer was heart-wrenching. "Yes," she said. "There was a bad man shooting." I reflected on my own childhood and the many times my parents asked, "How was school today?" Not once did I have to say, "There was a bad man shooting."

Active-shooter drills in American schools are now as routine as math and reading. What trauma are we visiting upon our children when we tell them that the best we can do for them is to teach them how to run and hide? As Highland Park parade shooting survivor Ashbey Beasley put it, "Every day we expect kids to go back to learning in classrooms where they have piled up desks to barricade doors." Some call the American obsession with guns freedom. But it is a strange freedom that routinely sends our children into lockdowns. That is the exact opposite of freedom. It is death.

During the vigil at Apalachee High School, one of my congressional colleagues applauded the school system's emergency response system, which included an armed on-site security officer, and seemed to suggest this hardening of schools as a model for these soft targets, as if that were sufficient and all we can do. If we apply that logic, are we going to harden every school in America, every grocery store? What about shopping malls? Spas? What about medical clinics? Houses of worship? Is that the answer? To turn the whole country into a fort, just so fourteen-year-olds can have AR-15s? As I said that day, we may not all agree on what to do about gun violence, but surely we can do better than that.

While mass shootings are dramatic in their impact on us, they make up just a tiny fraction of the gun violence that occurs each year in this country. In 2024, a total of 41,033 people died of all kinds of gun violence, according to the Gun Violence Archive. Of those deaths, 16,877 were due to homicide, murder, accidental discharges, or incidents in which people reportedly were defending themselves or others or their property. But more than half of the total number of deaths, those of 24,156 people, resulted from suicide. We must strengthen our nation's mental health care infrastructure, fortify and support organic networks of compassion and care like the faith communities, schools, and youth centers where people already gather for affirmation and recreation, and find ways to limit access to guns among people who are struggling with mental health issues and are a threat to themselves and others.

This is the intention behind red flag laws, which I support. These laws, also called extreme-risk laws, enable family members, law enforcement officers, health care workers, educators, and in some cases even coworkers, depending on the law in each state, to file what is often called an extreme-risk protection order (ERPO). This can lead to a judge ordering an emergency ERPO, which immediately removes a gun from the person at risk, before the matter is heard in court. This usually occurs within seven to twenty-one days, where the judge can extend the order to up to a year. Twenty-one states and the

District of Columbia have implemented these laws, according to Everytown for Gun Safety, a gun control research and advocacy nonprofit group. These protective measures are saving lives. The Scriptures remind us that people of strong faith have a moral obligation to "bear the infirmities of the weak," to protect them when they need it most, even from themselves (Romans 15:1, KJV).

After suicide, the second-most-common type of gun-related death in America is murder. Across this nation, 17,927 people were shot to death in 2023, so many souls lost because a firearm ended up in the wrong hands. Often the victim is a domestic spouse or partner, most often a woman, in an abusive marriage or relationship. But more times than not, the victim is a young black man. Homicide is the leading cause of death for black boys and men from ages one to forty-five, and the vast majority of those murders are committed with guns. Young black men between the ages of eighteen and twenty-four are nearly twenty-three times more likely to be shot to death than their white counterparts. These killings happen in poor black and brown communities every day, and they are no less tragic than the loss of lives in school shootings. As someone who has served in parish ministry in the urban centers of New York, Baltimore, and Atlanta, I've seen how these deaths are too casually dismissed as "black-on-black crime" because black faces are on both sides of the gun.

The grim truth is that white victims of homicide are just as likely to have been killed by someone of their own race, because most homicides are intraracial. Yet we never hear white murders referred to as "white-on-white" crime. I've seen how generational poverty, joblessness, marginalization, and despair often mix in these urban neighborhoods to create a combustible atmosphere of anger, self-hatred, and destruction. Throw in easy access to guns, and you have the same sad scenario playing out day after day in city after city.

What kind of nation countenances the murder of its young and says, "There is nothing we can do about that"? They are all somebody's children. They are all God's children. They are all *our* children. And we must never lose hope that we can implement the kind of change that will make life better for them and for us all.

> Even youths grow tired and weary, and young men stumble and fall; but those who hope in the Lord will renew their strength. They will soar on wings like eagles; they will run and not grow weary, they will walk and not be faint. (Isaiah 40:30–31, NIV)

Gun violence has a particular resonance at Ebenezer Baptist Church, where, in 1974, six years after Martin Luther King Jr. was shot to death, his mother, Alberta Williams King, was shot and killed inside the church. She was seated at the organ, playing "The Lord's Prayer," when a twenty-three-year-old deranged black man unloaded every round of the two handguns he held, killing both Mrs. King and a deacon. If the shooter had been carrying the kind of automatic weapons that so many mentally disturbed people have access to today, the carnage would have been far greater. The guns have gotten only more lethal, and access to mental health services has not gotten any better. Every day we live in a reality where any one of us could be in a mall, grocery store, school, or movie theater and be sprayed like insects.

We can and should do more about the proliferation of guns in this country—guns that too often end up in the wrong hands. In the United States of America, there are more guns than people. For every 100 American residents, there are 120 civilian-held firearms—the highest rate of any country in the world and double the rate of the next-highest country, according to a 2018 report by the Small Arms Survey, a research group based in Switzerland. We are awash in a sea of guns.

These days, with the advancement of 3D printing technology, you can even make guns at home. An increasing number of people are ordering the pieces online as do-it-yourself kits that can be assembled nearly as easily as a piece of mail-order furniture. They are called ghost guns because they initially were not stamped with serial numbers, which made them untraceable. Their component parts can be printed using 3D printers, and once assembled, they are as deadly as any other comparable firearm. It is no surprise that these ghost guns have become popular among criminals. When twenty-six-year-old Luigi Mangione was arrested and charged in the murder of UnitedHealthcare CEO Brian Thompson in December 2024, a ghost gun was found in his backpack, police said.

In 2022, under the Biden administration, the Bureau of Alcohol, Tobacco, Firearms and Explosives (ATF) began trying to regulate ghost guns. The agency redefined parts of the federal Gun Control Act of 1968 to hold these homemade guns to the same regulatory standard as other guns. The act generally requires manufacturers to add a serial number to every gun and dealers to conduct background checks and keep records of gun sales. But a group of gun owners, a gun components manufacturer, and gun advocates challenged the regulation. The legal challenge worked its way to the U.S. Supreme Court, which in March 2025 upheld the Biden administration's authority to regulate the homemade guns. The 7–2 decision saw four of the high court's conservative justices join three of its liberal members in a vote that was a major victory for gun safety.

Nevertheless, this is the same Supreme Court that in June 2024 invalidated the ATF's ban on bump stocks, a device that modifies a semiautomatic rifle to fire like a machine gun, in some cases between four hundred and eight hundred rounds per minute. Bump stocks catapulted into the national spotlight after they were found among the large cache of weapons and supplies in the hotel room of a man who slaughtered sixty people and wounded hundreds of others attending a country music festival on October 1, 2017, in Las Vegas. The shooter fired repeatedly from his thirty-second-floor hotel room window and then turned his gun on himself. This was the country's deadliest mass shooting by a single person. Afterward, the ATF refined existing federal law to include a ban on bump stocks beginning in 2019. But the Supreme Court decision five years later put the devices right back on the streets. So in court decisions and policies on gun safety, we seem to take one step back for every forward move, ultimately getting us nowhere.

Meanwhile, our streets are still flooded with guns. This is so despite the success of the Brady Act. The law is named in honor of James "Jim" Brady, President Ronald Reagan's former press secretary, who was shot in the head and partially paralyzed during an assassination attempt on the president in 1981. Jim Brady and his wife, Sarah, both Republicans and gun owners at the time, soon afterward joined the organization that now bears their last name and became tireless advocates for gun violence prevention. They lobbied Congress for six years before the act was passed and signed into law by President Bill Clinton in November 1993. It went into effect the next year, requiring federally licensed gun dealers to conduct background checks for the first time. Over the three-plus decades since, the law has blocked 4.9 million people from purchasing a firearm, according to the Brady organization. But the organization admits a gaping loophole in the law, which does not cover gun sales at popular gun shows or through private transactions, whether in person or online. One in five guns are sold this way, Brady says. So the fight continues.

Twenty-two states and the District of Columbia have extended their background-check requirement beyond those required by federal law to some gun sales from unlicensed individuals, and nineteen of those states and the District of Columbia require background checks for all gun sales, according to Giffords, a gun violence prevention organization founded by former Congresswoman Gabrielle Giffords, who was shot in the head at a "Congress on Your Corner" event for her constituents on January 8, 2011, in Tucson, Arizona. She survived, but six people died in the shooting, and twelve others were injured.

Congress could close that wide loophole with a federal law requiring universal background checks. Polls show that most Americans, across party lines, support some form of universal background checks. For all our differences, and they are real and deep, there is more agreement among Americans regarding gun safety than we have been led to believe. There is certainly more agreement than what is reflected in our current laws. Most Americans are dismayed by the everyday news of gun violence. We are stunned by the fact that since 2020 guns are now the number one cause of death for children and teenagers in America. In national polls, many of us cite gun violence as our number one public health concern. According to a Fox News poll (yes, Fox News!) a whopping 87 percent of Americans believe that universal background checks should be required for gun ownership. Yet the issue in recent years has not even been able to get a vote in Congress. If the people say overwhelmingly that they want good, commonsense safety measures like universal background checks, but Congress won't even address it, we must demand to know why. In large measure, it is because of the crooked places in our politics. Despite the people's pain and disapproval, our country is awash in guns because our political system is awash in money. Too many of our politicians are owned by corporate special interests like the gun lobby, and the people's voices are being squeezed out of their own democracy. This happens at both the federal and the state levels of our politics.

In 2023, after a mass shooter attacked the Covenant School, a private Christian elementary school in Nashville, Tennessee, killing three nine-year-olds and three adults, a small group of mothers began pushing for gun safety in a state dominated by Republicans. The state's governor is Republican, and Republicans hold a supermajority in the legislature. Likewise, the three mothers, whose children attended the Covenant School, were Republicans and supporters of the Second Amendment. They heard about a gun protest at their state capitol and decided to go; they were certain their fellow party members would hear their concerns and act. But they were wrong.

I'm not surprised, because long before taking office as a U.S. senator, I often trudged over to the state capitol in Georgia with other clergy members and faith leaders to advocate for commonsense gun-safety laws. It always amazed me how year after year, the gun lobby would come back with new propositions to make sure more people had more access to more powerful guns. Despite the distortions of this debate by demagogues, we sought safety, not the seizure of everybody's guns. On the other hand, the corporate gun lobby and its enablers wanted guns in restaurants and bars. They wanted guns in schools and government buildings. They wanted guns in airports. I remember how each time they got what they wanted, they would turn around and come right back to get some more. In fact, Georgia is now known as the "guns everywhere" state. Ironically, though, each time I and other clergy visited the state capitol, we had to go through metal detectors to meet with our state leaders, who apparently wanted guns everywhere *except* in their own place of work.

I'm always struck by the immense passion that some people have for guns. After the horrible school shooting in Uvalde, I spent some time with U.S. Representative Tony Gonzales, one of the Republican legislators who has represented Uvalde in Congress since 2021. Gonzales, then a freshman legislator, shared with me that as he met with family members of the victims, a relative of a little girl who was killed made a special plea: "Don't let them take our guns away!" Even in his grief, the relative worried that Congress might try to take his guns.

A month after the shooting, Gonzales, a moderate who believes, as I do, in building bridges across party lines, would take a brave step that angered fellow Republicans back home. Gonzales broke with most in his party and became the only Republican from Texas in the House of Representatives to vote in favor of the landmark Bipartisan Safer Communities Act. He told a local newspaper that his vote was inspired in part by the childhood experience of watching his stepfather threaten his mother with a gun. "As a congressman it's my duty to pass laws that never infringe on the Constitution while protecting the lives of the innocent," he wrote on Twitter days before the vote. But for sticking his hand up to vote on a meaningful bipartisan bill that was sponsored by a fellow Texas legislator—U.S. Senator John Cornyn, the senior Texas Republican in the Senate—Gonzales was censured by the Republican Party of Texas. In a broken system where dark money talks loudly, it takes guts to be an independent thinker in the legislature.

On another occasion, a few years before my election to the Senate, I was living in Ormewood Park, just east of downtown Atlanta, next door to a young couple with a toddler and another baby on the way. One morning, the husband asked if he could use my driveway. He explained that his family was moving out and it would be easier to reverse the van from my side. I agreed, and as I stood there watching him load boxes, I had to do a double take. Honestly, I didn't know my neighbor well. The family hadn't lived there long. He was a lawyer, an unassuming guy, living with his family in a relatively safe neighborhood. To my amazement, he suddenly strolled outside with an AR-15. The casual way he carted it off haunts me. It was as if the gun were just one more item, no more meaningful than an armchair. I looked at him with a kind of sideways expression. "Is that what I think it is?" I asked. His expression was nonchalant, as if to respond, "Why not?"

My daughter, then two years old, was inside. I remember thinking, "This guy was right next to us the whole time." *With an AR-15.* And this isn't just a weapon that kills people. It's a weapon that renders children utterly unrecognizable.

The casual handling and display of these types of guns stuns me. When I see congressional representatives and elected officials send out Christmas cards with their families and even their children displaying semiautomatic weapons, I can't help wondering how this message could possibly honor the spirit of Christmas.

I don't know what my neighbor's politics were. However, I

do understand that there's a sense among many on the right that they are under siege. I understand that a good number of them believe they're a religious minority whose worldview is under assault by secularists on the left who are out to get them. They may be living in a media echo chamber that constantly emphasizes crime in a nation that is actually safer than it once was. Hence they feel the need for guns everywhere.

The empathetic side of me wants to remember that there's a way in which we all have building blocks of meaning that we create just to maintain our sanity and to be able to function in the world. We all wake up with a certain set of assumptions that allow us to navigate through society. And when things are constantly being thrown at us that upset those assumptions, or when we see too much change happening too fast, we become afraid. We should use this insight to be a little more patient with our neighbors and to turn the temperature down in our conversations about the issues on which we disagree, like gun safety, and about the future of the country.

As a man of faith and a pastor, I believe there's room around God's big table for all the people, with all our differences. I didn't grow up hunting and using real guns for recreation as a child. But my father was a veteran and a patriot who flew the American flag in our small church, where he preached, and he imbued in me a deep love of this country, despite its flaws. I support the Constitution's Second Amendment. Hunters ought to be able to hunt. But do you really need an AR-15? We have differences in this country, but we must make the gun issue less about culture and more about safety, in a way akin to what we did with seat belts in a nation that loves its cars. After all, polls have shown that there is plenty of common ground where we can stand together. Together we are mightier. So let's find that common ground and stand together. Ordinary citizens, particularly parents. Parents who are tired of our children dying. Parents who are tired of feeling helpless about it. Parents who are tired of standing by as nothing gets done. We may be on opposite sides of the political spectrum and disagree on a whole range of subjects, but we must come together to create an unlikely and inclusive coalition to push the issue of gun safety forward.

And the movement must start with the people. As an elected official, I find it shameful that Americans cannot count on so many of the people they elected to public office, because the politicians' ears are tuned only to the lobbyists. In my home state, for example, the conventional wisdom is that if you're a Democratic elected official you're going to have to at least triangulate on the gun issue to be successful. Politicians look at the odds and calculate that they haven't a snowball's chance in hell without support from the gunmakers. But then, here I stand, proof of the promise of January 5, 2021. How is it that I was elected as the first black senator ever to represent

Georgia, even though the National Rifle Association, for decades the largest, most influential gun lobbyist, consistently gave me an "F" rating? My response to the organization, by the way, is "Can I get an 'F minus'?"

The gun lobby floods Washington with money, and in the chambers of government, through which change can happen, there is only silence. It is our moral responsibility to acknowledge that much of the daily violence we see in our communities is fueled by greed and political opportunism. Gun lobbyists spread their wealth across Congress and state legislatures, buy loyalty and fear, and tuck elected officials into their pockets. Our broken political system of legalized bribery is blocking commonsense gun-safety reforms and fueling unspeakable pain and destruction. Thus, we cannot get significant movement on critical gun-safety issues, like universal background checks, even when ordinary Americans on both sides of the aisle overwhelmingly agree on them. Instead, after every mass shooting this past decade, stock prices for gun companies shot upward. Since 2021, gun and ammunition companies have seen profits rise in the billions.

These are among the crooked places that must be made straight. They are the rough places that must be made smooth. And we, the people, must do it. We must come together and use our collective strength to demand integrity and change. For far too long, we have sat idly, feeling helpless and hopeless, watching school shooting after school shooting and young people dying in our cities and towns. We have been in hiding. Hiding behind our fears. Hiding behind cultural myths about power and might. What does our inability to act say about us as a people? That we are morally weak and spiritually broken? Or perhaps, as in the words of Isaiah, "the whole head is sick, and the whole heart faint" (Isaiah 1:5, KJV). Yet I gain strength and hope when I reflect on the times in our nation's history when a seemingly intractable wrong has been made right. I think of the women's suffrage movement and the long journey from that first women's rights convention at Seneca Falls, New York, in 1848, to the Nineteenth Amendment in 1920, giving women the right to vote. A rough place made smooth.

As I see it, working together to make our communities safer is God's work. I find confidence in the assurance that God gave Isaiah. We, too, can take heart, knowing that this work is for a righteous cause and thus we are not alone.

> So do not fear, for I am with you; do not be dismayed,
> for I am your God. I will strengthen you and help you;
> I will uphold you with my righteous right hand.
> (Isaiah 41:10, NIV)

6

HUMBLE OURSELVES, HEAL THE LAND

As I reflected on the twentieth anniversary of Hurricane Katrina in August 2025, I couldn't help but think of what a sober reminder it was that we must take better care of this beautiful earth that God has loaned to us. Scripture reminds us that "the earth is the Lord's and all that is in it, the world, and those who live in it" (Psalms 24:1, NRSVA). Yes, all of it and all of us belong to God, and we are therefore called upon to be good stewards.

By now, we know—or should know—that much of the damage caused by Hurricane Katrina was preventable. All that death and destruction, around 1,400 lives lost and $125 billion in property and structural damage, didn't have to happen at such a tragic scale. Scientists had warned for years that the wetlands along coastal Louisiana needed to be protected and restored because they were vanishing and taking with them nature's buffer against the surge from a superstorm.

Louisiana has lost over a million acres of wetlands. And the biggest culprits, according to Ivor van Heerden, one of the nation's leading experts on hurricanes, are the oil and gas industries and their drilling and dredging activities along the coast. From its first successful oil well drilling in a rice field in southwestern Louisiana in 1901, the industry quickly expanded, providing a huge boost to the state's economy. By the 1960s, the oil and gas industry accounted for 60 percent of the state's total revenues, according to a 2024 report by the Institute for Energy Economics and Financial Analysis. The industry's share of the state's revenues had declined to 40 percent by the late 1990s. But still, at the turn of the twenty-first century, Louisiana had one of the fastest-growing economies in the nation, thanks in considerable part to its oil and gas companies. Today the scenario has completely flipped. The industry currently provides just 4.5 percent of the state's revenues, and Louisiana has the second-worst-growing economy, according to the same report, "The Declining Significance of the Petrochemical Industry in Louisiana." The report found that the state is still overly reliant on a declining industry and recommends that officials find new areas and systems of growth. But the money trail offers some clue about how the industry wielded such power in the state for so long.

Van Heerden, former deputy director of the Hurricane Center at Louisiana State University, says the state's petrochemical industries are responsible for the bulk of the wetlands loss in coastal Louisiana. "When I initially arrived in the seventies to do my graduate studies, south and east and west of New Orleans were huge cypress swamps, and for thousands of years the best protection from hurricanes that we've had were these coastal wetlands," he told National Geographic in a televised special documentary recognizing the twentieth anniversary of Hurricane Katrina. "But it didn't take me long to realize that Louisiana is losing its wetlands at a hell of a rate, including the wetlands around the Lower Ninth Ward and St. Bernard."

When Hurricane Katrina hit on August 29, 2005, those were two of the hardest-hit areas.

We all watched in horror and helplessness as this epic storm slammed into New Orleans, breaking the levees and leaving most of the city underwater. And the people who couldn't get out beforehand were left fighting for their lives at home by climbing into attics or onto rooftops. Or they ended up among the tens of thousands of people stuck at the Superdome or the Ernest N. Morial Convention Center without adequate food or water in squalid, putrid conditions. They were New Orleans's poorest people, and most of them were black.

The timing of Hurricane Katrina is also particularly memorable for me because I was transitioning into my new role as pastor of Ebenezer. Two months earlier, I had been elected as the new pastor, but I had not yet moved to Atlanta to begin. The congregation contributed money for the more than 100,000 New Orleanians who had evacuated to Atlanta. When I arrived in October 2005, we also sent our youth ministry team to help with a cleanup mission in the city. But my first major social action as the new pastor was to organize and lead the Freedom Caravan, which included several coach buses that transported hundreds of the displaced residents back home to New Orleans in April 2006 to vote in the primary election of a controversial mayor's race. A month later, we transported the voters back to New Orleans for the runoff between two Democrats—the black incumbent, Ray Nagin, who had been a political newcomer when he was first elected to the office in 2002, and then–Louisiana Lieutenant Governor Mitch Landrieu, who came from a prominent white political family that included his father, a former New Orleans mayor, and his sister, a U.S. senator at the time. Hurricane Katrina already had taken so much from these displaced residents. We wanted to make sure that bureaucratic indifference and the racial politics swirling after the storm didn't take away these citizens' voices or their votes.

Part of what Hurricane Katrina put vividly on display was

the vulnerability of our poor during a disaster. But every day, the most vulnerable members of our human family face disproportionately higher levels of danger from toxins in the built environment. The same fossil fuel and petrochemical industries that have been causing such destruction to the wetlands in Louisiana are polluting the air and water in an eighty-five-mile stretch along the Mississippi River between New Orleans and Baton Rouge, known as Cancer Alley. From 150 to 200 petrochemical and fossil fuel production plants operate along that stretch, and communities located alongside them have some of the highest rates of cancer in the country. They also face significantly increased risks of reproductive health issues, birth defects, and respiratory illnesses. Some of these plants and facilities were built on the sites of former sugar cane plantations, and many of those who live and work there are generational descendants of the enslaved people who once toiled in those fields.

The federal Environmental Protection Agency's own studies show the disproportionate cancer risk that black residents in this part of southeastern Louisiana face from industrial air pollution. The EPA even urged Louisiana health and environmental officials in 2022 to relocate children from one predominantly black elementary school in St. John the Baptist Parish because the school was exposed to a dangerous carcinogen at levels eleven times what the federal agency considers acceptable. (After community pressure, a lawsuit, and the school board voting to shut down the school by summer 2025, the chemical manufacturer agreed to halt production at its nearby facility.)

Concerns about the conditions along Cancer Alley in Louisiana had already gotten the attention of a group of independent experts appointed by the United Nations Human Rights Council. In March 2021, they released a statement condemning what had been happening along that dangerous corridor as environmental racism. "The African American descendants of the enslaved people who once worked the land are today the primary victims of deadly environmental pollution that these petrochemical plants in their neighborhoods have caused," the human rights observers said. They expressed concern about further industrialization in the region and called upon the United States to "pay reparations for the centuries of harm to Afro-descendants rooted in slavery and colonization."

The more I look at the often-dismal life chances of poor children, especially those living in environmentally ravaged communities, the more clearly I see the link between poverty and the environment. This connection, while not often recognized in our public discourse, is not new. Dr. Robert Bullard, the "father of environmental justice," who was inducted into the American Academy of Arts and Sciences in 2023, has been writing about and active in the movement against environmental racism since the 1980s.

In Louisiana, local activists have been fighting for decades to be heard. But in 2023, three faith-based groups of black activists came together in St. James Parish, a jurisdiction within Cancer Alley, and filed an environmental racism lawsuit in federal court against the parish council. The lawsuit contended that for the past forty-six years the St. James Parish Council has approved new industrial plants in majority-black neighborhoods in the parish while "explicitly sparing" majority-white neighborhoods. While infuriating and heartbreaking, the claims were hardly surprising.

We, as a society, have long known that race is the most significant predictor of where a toxic dump, hazardous chemical plant, or other facility that no one else wants will be placed. We've known that black children have higher rates of asthma than white children, in part because of where they live. They are more likely to miss school, end up in the hospital, or even die from asthma. We've known, too, that poor black and brown children suffer from disproportionately higher incidences of poisoning from lead and other toxins found in the antiquated housing units where they live. These dangerous toxins cause an array of problems, from extreme learning challenges to behavioral issues to fast-tracked entry into the criminal system. We've known all of this, and yet we are not talking to one another in the spirit of Isaiah's teachings and principles. If we were, the environmental justice movement would include every single living being on this planet.

We cannot continue to dismiss these environmental issues as someone else's problem. We are all impacted. The earth's climate is warming at a rate that hasn't been seen in the past ten thousand years, and humans are the cause, according to the Intergovernmental Panel on Climate Change, a United Nations body that is the premier authority on assessing the science related to climate change. "Since systematic scientific assessments began in the 1970s, the influence of human activities on the warming of the climate system has evolved from theory to established fact," according to the contributors to the IPCC's Sixth Assessment Report.

The same fossil fuel industries that are destroying the wetlands, polluting the air and water, and making their neighbors desperately ill in Louisiana's Cancer Alley and elsewhere have been worsening global warming. Experts tell us that the burning of these fossil fuels (oil, coal, and gas) produces over 75 percent of the greenhouse gas emissions that lead to global warming and climate change. These gas emissions trap more of the sun's energy in the earth system, and the extra energy warms the atmosphere, ocean, and land. The average surface temperature of the planet has risen about two degrees Fahrenheit since the late nineteenth century, with most of the warming occurring in the past forty years, NASA says. The agency's satellites show that spring snow cover in the Northern Hemisphere has decreased over the past five decades, and snow is melting earlier. Across this nation, we've seen other dramatic results: dangerous heat waves, ravaging wildfires in Southern California, scary storm surges, superstorms, deadly flooding in unusual places, and more, all of which can be traced to global warming.

God's verdant green earth is talking. Loudly.

Yet we go about our lives as if we have forever to change course. The agriculture sector is among the biggest polluters in the U.S., contributing around 10 percent of greenhouse gas emissions. This means that if we really wanted to help the planet, we'd all put down our burgers and simply become vegetarians. I chuckle here because I am not quite willing to do that, and I'd venture to say that most people are not. But what *can* we do? What sacrifices can we make to address such an urgent existential crisis?

Isaiah warns us of the deadly consequences of doing nothing:

> The earth dries up and withers, the world languishes and withers; the heavens languish together with the earth. The earth lies polluted under its inhabitants; for they have transgressed laws, violated the statutes, broken the everlasting covenant. Therefore, a curse

> devours the earth, and its inhabitants suffer for their guilt; therefore the inhabitants of the earth dwindled, and few people are left. (Isaiah 24:4–6, NRSVUE)

I first started to focus on the climate emergency (although we didn't call it that yet) as a graduate student at Union Theological Seminary in New York in the 1990s, where I began to think about the threat in terms of Christian ethical implications. I learned to ask, what was our responsibility as stewards of creation?

In the years since then, I've come to find countless connections between the climate crisis and the need for Isaiah's moral topography. During my first years at Ebenezer, I looked for ways to engage the issue directly. While there were people in the church who cared deeply about the issue, the ministry as a body had not yet focused on climate justice in a sustained way. I decided that this was an issue we needed to address as an urgent moral crisis. In 2009, we launched Earth Day Sunday—renamed Creation Care Sunday in 2023—on Earth Day weekend, and in my inaugural sermon I made the same argument that I have continued to make in the years since, which is this: The crisis of environmental disaster has too often been framed as a white, upper-middle-class issue. The movement simply has not done a good job at diversifying its ranks. People who care most about the environment also need to be saying a whole lot more about civil rights and justice. At the same time, many of my own friends who speak in such a powerful way about civil rights need to be saying a whole lot more about the environment. There is no greater human right than the right to breathe clean air and drink clean water. Environmental activists and civil rights activists need to build strong multiracial and multigenerational coalitions for a movement that will transform our country and save the planet.

That was the goal in March 2019 when I joined former Vice President Al Gore and the Reverend Dr. William J. Barber II for a big, interfaith meeting on climate justice at my church. I was happy to partner with both men—Gore, who began sounding the climate crisis alarm long before many folks were listening, and Barber, a preacher and longtime civil rights activist who the year before co-led the relaunch of the Poor People's Campaign first envisioned by Dr. King. Both men understand the urgency of activists with intersecting interests working together, and our meeting, "A Moral Call to Action on the Climate Crisis," drew a crowd that packed the church to capacity. It was held as part of a broader three-day series of climate activism and environmental justice training by the Climate Reality Leadership Corps, which is operated by Gore's Climate Reality Project.

"What is going on in the public square right now is more important than any time since the Civil War," Gore said then. "We are facing an ecological crisis that can bring about the end of civilization."

As a nation, we should have listened to Gore when he first warned about global warming in 1981 as a U.S. representative who organized the first congressional hearing on global warming. I've continued to find ways to partner on environmental issues, and in recent years, as part of Creation Care Sunday, Ebenezer has joined my friend Reverend Dr. Heber Brown III and his innovative Black Church Food Security Network. The group guides member congregations, an alliance of nearly 250 churches throughout much of the country, in growing environmentally sound gardens on their land, buying wholesale from black farmers, and hosting miniature farmers markets using the labor and skills of their members. The goal is to create black-owned food systems that protect the environment and serve the needs of the community. Brown was pastor of Pleasant Hope Baptist Church in Baltimore in 2010, when he and his congregation started a community garden, growing corn, broccoli, kale, tomatoes, strawberries, herbs, and more behind the church. He soon recognized that in a majority-black city with vast food deserts that he deemed "food apartheid," black churches were not engaged on that issue. He set out to change that, connecting black churches and black farmers to bring fresh food to the people. In 2015, Brown officially established the nonprofit Black Church Food Security Network, and within a few years, congregations beyond Baltimore had come on board. After fourteen years as pastor of Pleasant Hope, he resigned to focus on this new calling full time.

I am proud that as part of Brown's network, Ebenezer started our own food co-op with a regular farmers market. Community members can come to our church after service on certain Sundays and buy turnip greens, yams, and other produce directly from farmers. Heber Brown is working to push the faith community out of its comfort zone and into these agrarian and sustainability spaces. He's also working in the proud tradition of Vernon Johns, who preceded Dr. King as pastor of Dexter Avenue Baptist Church in Montgomery, Alabama. Johns was a brilliant academic and a prophetic figure who was as much a farmer as a fiery preacher. He stirred up good trouble with his contrarian ideas and sermons, challenging the status quo in segregated 1940s and '50s Alabama. His messages made his upper-crust congregants uncomfortable, as did his antics. He often pulled up in front of the church with a truck full of fresh collard greens and turnips from his garden for sale. Sometimes he even stepped into the pulpit in his overalls and boots, fresh from plowing his crops. All of this might have seemed just a bit too unrefined and "country" for the relatively highbrow congregation of Dexter Avenue Baptist Church, made up of professors from Alabama State, the local HBCU, and the class consciousness and sensibilities of others of the black bourgeoisie beholden to the politics of respectability. Moreover, he was an outspoken activist who championed racial justice with the kind of prophetic fire that needled the segregationist establishment of Montgomery with provocative sermon titles placed each week on the church marquee. After a spree of killings of black men by white police officers in Alabama were all ruled to be justifiable homicide, Johns took to his pulpit to preach a sermon titled "It Is Safe to Murder Negroes in Montgomery." Johns urged his congregants to stand up and resist violence and injustice. He was pushed to resign, as the congregation hoped for a less radical leader. They chose a twenty-five-year-old graduate student who was still finishing up his PhD at Boston University. Surely, many probably thought, he would not rock the boat. His name was Dr. Martin Luther King Jr.

As a senator, I see how the climate emergency has become increasingly urgent and life-threatening, with the potential to alter our way of life much sooner than we think.

Together with my colleague Jon Ossoff, I was the lead sponsor of a bill that incentivized the domestic production of solar panels. The bill became part of the 2022 Inflation Reduction Act, which was the federal government's largest investment in clean energy and clean-energy jobs in U.S. history. In Georgia alone, clean-energy businesses announced fifty-one new projects worth $28 billion. The manufacturing projects, producing batteries, solar panels, electric vehicles, and more, are expected to generate forty-two thousand new jobs. That includes many well-paying positions that don't require a college degree. For every dollar of federal investment in Georgia, the state saw $4.50 in private investment. That is a good deal. It shows that the market will respond positively when we take bold steps toward producing clean energy. It shows that taking care of our environment is good business and that ecological and economic stability are inextricably linked, not opposing objectives. We should be doing more of this work, not less. It is about investing in a future worthy of our children.

Sustainability is soul work. And I'm proud that my home state of Georgia is leading the way. In Dalton, Georgia, for example, a South Korean clean-energy company called Qcells, which manufactures solar panels, completed a massive expansion project that enabled the factory to manufacture nearly thirty thousand solar panels a day. This company in tiny Dalton, Georgia, known, because it produces 75 percent of the world's carpets, as the "Carpet Capital of the World," is now the largest manufacturer of solar panels in the Western Hemisphere. Near my hometown of Savannah, a new Hyundai plant is building electric vehicles, poised to create another 8,500 jobs. These companies and others are creating clean energy *and* clean-energy jobs. This is what can and must be done to respond to the environmental crisis facing our country and ensure a thriving, sustainable future.

In addition to its clean-energy investments, the Inflation Reduction Act included significant financing incentives for farmers to help make their processes more sustainable. Our farmers are the answer to our prayers: "Give us this day our daily bread." They have seen close up the destruction caused by severe weather patterns that are the result of climate change. I've stood with them in the wake of some of those disasters, and as a member of the Senate Committee on Agriculture, Nutrition, and Forestry, I have put forth legislation to provide safety-net programs for specialty crops and make it easier for farmers whose crops are destroyed by extreme weather to receive disaster relief. These are issues that ultimately touch all our lives, so they should not be as partisan as they are most days.

I have been particularly gratified to work with a few of my Republican colleagues on bipartisan legislation that both assists our farmers and protects our environment. I worked with

Majority Leader John Thune of South Dakota to introduce the Promoting Precision Agriculture Act. Precision agriculture uses new technologies to make farming safer, more sustainable, and more economically efficient using highly sophisticated sensors, artificial intelligence, robots, drones, and tractors that don't look like our granddads' tractors. These technologies help farmers to be more efficient in the use of water, fertilizer, and pesticides so that dangerous chemicals are not overused. Among other things, our legislation directs key federal agencies to develop "voluntary, consensus-based, industry-led interconnectivity standards, guidelines, and best practices" to encourage adoption of these technologies. This is the kind of bipartisan cooperation that is needed to find visionary solutions to save our planet. It does not happen often enough. Most times, we are fighting against one another, as if we do not share the destiny of our planet.

We all need to do much more, and much more quickly than we can even imagine. That is why I find it so disheartening, even infuriating, that the current Trump administration and my Republican colleagues are playing politics, undermining the progress we've made toward securing our children's and our grandchildren's futures on this planet. In Georgia, 83 percent of the new clean-energy projects, 94 percent of the total investment, and 75 percent of the jobs were in Republican districts. These investments were going to areas that are so often overlooked, including lower-income counties and counties where people are less likely to have a college degree. But the sad truth is that some of our politicians are so cynical that they wanted to do away with the legislation just because it was passed by a Democratic Congress and signed into law by a Democratic president. They are so focused on politics that they're willing to hurt their own people. And the story is not exclusive to Georgia. We might be a leader in the clean-energy economy, but we are all in this together. Our nationwide project to create an economy that protects our climate takes all of us.

But on the first day of his second term, President Trump paused all grants, disbursements, and loans under the Inflation Reduction Act and suspended approval of new renewable wind-energy projects. He also revoked Biden's electric vehicle mandate, aimed at supporting the adoption of electric vehicles. His administration has even proposed reversing federal regulations that cap greenhouse gas pollution from cars and other vehicles. And his big, ugly bill, which was rammed through Congress by the Republican majority, rolled back many of the Inflation Reduction Act's clean-energy incentives. These steps have had a devastating economic impact, with businesses pulling back billions in clean-energy investments. How can a businessman who wrote a book to show others the art of deal-making refuse to see that his collective actions are a bad deal for the American people? His big, ugly bill leaned into the resources of yesterday, like coal, instead of embracing green technologies that will power us into the future, like wind and solar. This mindset puts our country at a competitive disadvantage around the world. China already far outpaces the United States with its production of 70 percent of the world's supply of electric cars, the vehicles of the future. Shortsighted, partisan thinking sets the framework for an America that no longer leads the world but cedes its place to China and is eventually left behind.

But here's the worst part about President Trump's antagonistic stance toward clean energy: It is deaf to the cries of an imperiled earth. It is arrogantly dismissive of our moral obligation to be good stewards of God's creation.

President Trump's withdrawal from the Paris climate agreement was like a middle finger to a world that came together in 2015 and agreed that we owe it to our planet to do better. All 195 United Nations members who attended its 2015 UN Climate Change Conference, including then-President Barack Obama, signed the global agreement to battle climate change by addressing global warming. Each nation committed to set its own targets for reducing greenhouse gas emissions with periodic updates. The participation of the United States and China, which also signed the agreement, was crucial because they are the world's largest polluters, accounting for around

40 percent of greenhouse gas emissions. But after Trump was elected to office, he decided to withdraw from the Paris agreement in 2017 at the urging of twenty-two Republican senators. Trump claimed that our country's ambitious goals to reduce greenhouse gas emissions would drive up costs and place American companies at a competitive disadvantage. President Biden restored our country's participation in the agreement during his time in office. But just hours after Trump took office for his second term in January 2025, he withdrew again, citing his "America first" agenda.

How does allowing manufacturers to continue poisoning Americans with impunity put America first? The whole notion that pulling out of the Paris agreement protects Americans is a fallacy—as much a fallacy as believing that we can have such a thing as an "America first" agenda when it comes to climate change. We breathe the same air. We share the same planet, and our destinies on it are intertwined. American lives are precious and worthy of protection, but they cannot be protected without also protecting the lives and human dignity of our brothers and sisters across the globe.

As the father of two young children, I, like so many others, worry deeply about their future in an environment that will bring massive natural disasters and unthinkable destabilization to their way of life. We're setting the stage and the terms for their very ability to survive. It is possible that they may even be denied so many of the simple pleasures that we take for granted, like strawberries and fresh salmon. Within a decade, this planet will have nine billion people to feed. How are we going to do that in a way that is sustainable? That is the question that should both terrify us and inspire us to act.

I know that many who have been in this fight a long time, as I have, are feeling discouraged, like we can't win. But here's what we cannot do: give up. We know that those who have chosen not to believe the science are attacking the work we've been doing. We know they're attacking the Inflation Reduction Act and those clean-energy credits. We know they're attacking the poor and health care and the health of the planet. But here's the other thing that they're doing. They're trying to weaponize despair. And whatever battles we may win or lose in the short term, this is the battle that we cannot afford to lose. We cannot allow those without a vision for a healthy planet and a healthy tomorrow to succeed in weaponizing despair and thereby convince us that they have already won. Because when you're convinced that they've already won, you lose hope. You give in and thereby guarantee defeat.

I am not about to give this planet, the only home we have, over to those who are so blinded by greed that they would sell our children short. I'm proud that I get to do this work. And even though I am an elected official, I am not in love with politics. I'm in love with change.

Many days I feel like I just put up with politics. And the reason I put up with politics is because every now and then we get to do something amazing, like pass the Inflation Reduction Act, the largest investment in clean energy in American history. So when I'm weary, I turn to my source for encouragement, and I'm reminded and reassured by these words: "Let us not become weary in doing good, for at the proper time we will reap a harvest if we do not give up" (Galatians 6:9, NIV).

So let us find the strength together to stay in the fight, to speak truth to power, to remind our brothers and sisters on this planet that, again, in the words of Dr. King, we are tied in a single garment of destiny. I have the great honor and privilege of standing every Sunday in the pulpit where Dr. King stood. I was pastor to the late, great Congressman John Lewis. I knew Reverend Joseph Lowery, and I hung out at his house all the time. Dr. King's sister, Christine, sat in the second row of our church listening to me preach until 2023, when she passed away. So I saw her every Sunday. These are giants of the civil rights movement. I'm sure there were times back then when the task ahead of them seemed impossible. But at times I can feel their spirit lifting my head, pulling my shoulders back, strengthening my resolve.

Former Ambassador Andrew Young is still with us. He once told me a story that I think about often these days. He said that a few months after the Civil Rights Act of 1964 was passed, Dr. King went with some of his lieutenants to the White House to meet with President Lyndon B. Johnson. Dr. King began to say to President Johnson, "Mr. President, we need a voting rights law. My people can't vote." Despite the passage of the Thirteenth, Fourteenth, and Fifteenth Amendments, one hundred years later, so many black people had no access to the ballot box. The president responded, "Martin, you don't understand. I can't get that done right now. I just passed the civil rights law. It took a whole lot of political capital. Took a whole lot just to get that over the finish line. I'm sorry, I just don't have the power."

According to Ambassador Young, Dr. King and his crew left the meeting, and the staff was feeling pretty demoralized and dejected. They asked, "Dr. King, what are we going to do? The president just said he doesn't have the power." Dr. King just sort of shrugged and said, "Well, if the president doesn't have the power to do it, I guess we're going to have to go down to the South and get the president some power."

So when you see those pictures from Selma, Alabama, when you see John Lewis and Hosea Williams crossing that bridge, when you see all those folks standing up to brute force, know that this is what they were doing. The president said he didn't have power. And so they went to get him some.

That's what we've got to do in this moral moment. The civil

rights activists. The environmental activists. People of goodwill across the globe. We've got to remember that it's not about the *people* in power. It is about the *power* that's in the people. We've got to fight for the planet. For our children. For generations yet unborn. We've got to keep pushing, keep praying, keep working.

We are all in this together. The prophet Isaiah reminds us, "And the glory of the Lord shall be revealed, and all flesh shall see it *together*: for the mouth of the Lord hath spoken *it*" (Isaiah 40:5, KJV).

CODA

Monrovia, Liberia, August 28, 2025. A church mission trip brought me to this struggling little nation on the Atlantic coast of West Africa. As I move through its streets and see faces that look like mine and street names that sound as American as any back home, I can't help but reflect on how this place is also a part of our complex American story. Its first settlers were freeborn or formerly enslaved in the United States but were transported here as part of a "repatriation" experiment some two hundred years ago, as an American nation conceived in liberty wrestled, in varying ways, through the complexities and contradictions of slavery. The establishment of this new nation was one response.

Its name, Liberia, meaning "land of the free," was given to it by the American Colonization Society, an organization whose history and motivations are as complicated as the American project itself and its enduring racial dilemma. Nonetheless, the name Liberia expresses the earnest yearning of those new settlers. They eventually would even name this capital city in honor of James Monroe, the fifth president of the United States and a supporter of the repatriation. Liberia's charter documents—its Constitution and Declaration of Independence—signed at the Providence Baptist Church, where I preached earlier this week, echo the ideals of freedom in America's Constitution and Declaration of Independence. Chasing those ideals has not been easy. Over time, Liberia has been ravaged by civil war, political conflicts, and health crises, including a devastating Ebola outbreak. Yet in spite of its long and complicated history with America, in many ways, it remains in pursuit of the idealism and hope that have made America great. That is a paradox known on both sides of the Atlantic.

I, too, still believe in America.

Our grand cathedral is 250 years in the making. It is majestic, mighty, and full of possibility; yet it remains unfinished. At a time when our country is so deeply divided, I urge us to recognize the danger of our divisions, of allowing demagogues with no vision to deepen the chasm and tear down what has been built with blood and sacrifice. I urge us instead to lean toward the moral work that can and must be done and to ask ourselves what kind of nation we want. I urge us to imagine a future full of hope for everyone. The future Isaiah laid out so clearly:

> Every valley shall be exalted, and every mountain and hill brought low. The crooked places shall be made straight, and the rough places smooth. The glory of the Lord shall be revealed, and all flesh shall see it together. (Isaiah 40:4–5, NKJV)

At the heart of that ideal is equity. *Every* valley shall be exalted. It is indispensable to the American ideal and the foundation for a just and prosperous society. A society where we protect the vulnerable and take responsibility for building a path that honors the humanity of "the least of these." A society where all our children have access to good food, a solid education, and opportunities for a bright future. A society where all our children are safe and the planet that we leave them is sustainable.

We have less equity in our society because we have less integrity in our politics. We need more integrity in our political process. Our political system is awash in money, the sources of a lot of which are dark and hidden. Campaign finance reform is among the most consequential issues we can be working on right now, because it speaks to who owns our democracy. It speaks to the question of whether we are a democracy or an oligarchy or a kleptocracy where increasingly the people's house is looted for self-enrichment by the powerful and well-connected. We will have more equity in our society when we have more integrity in our politics.

And this is precisely where most of us tune out, because the problems seem so insurmountable. They're simply far too heavy a load for the average person, who is just trying to make it through the day. I, too, get tired on this journey. I, too, suffer from physical, emotional, and spiritual fatigue. I think the entire country now registers a kind of low-grade fever, a vague and inexpressible weariness brought on by the sheer trauma of the assault on our democracy. In the meantime, demagogues who trade in hate, fear, unbridled corruption, and opportunism exploit our vulnerability by convincing us that we need to be afraid of each other.

Which America will we choose? The people of Georgia chose hope when they sent a boy who had to rely on the generosity of our government, via public housing, food stamps, Head Start, and Pell Grants, to represent them in the United States Senate. I am the embodiment of American possibility. I am the embodiment of the great hope of America. I center my work on kids like me. Symbolically, I ask those children today, "How are you doing, kid?" I'm afraid the answer today is not well, not full of hope.

In the Maasai culture of southern Kenya and northern Tanzania and in some parts of Ethiopia, the warriors greet one another with the phrase *Kasserian ingera*, which means "And how are the children?" I love it because it doesn't ask, "How are *your* children?" It instead inquires about the well-being of all children, the next generation. I long for an America that measures itself on the merits of that question: *And how are the children?* The gross domestic product, or GDP, the total market value of our country's goods and services, provides an incomplete picture of how our nation is doing. The Dow Jones Industrial Average and the New York Stock Exchange prices at the closing bell on Wall Street give us just a small, incomplete portrait. Viewed alone, either can give a distorted picture of how we are doing as a nation. If a nation is materially wealthy, as ours is, yet masses of its children are stuck on the opposite side of the divide without access to its multiplicity of resources, it is a nation that is spiritually poor. If America is to fully realize its greatness, we must center the children. We must consider the possibilities for the nation's poor, working-class, and middle-class families. Just as greed and injustice poison our politics, poverty and violence deplete our families.

Isaiah offers us a vision that at first blush seems improbable. "The wolf will live with the lamb, the leopard will lie down with the goat, and the calf and the lion and the yearling together; and a child shall lead them." Even for me, someone who has been preaching for the better part of my life, it took a while to understand the deeper meaning of that passage. But what Isaiah says is that even in a divided nation and a divided world, the thing that even mortal enemies have in common is this: We all love our children. The thing that we too seldom understand is that the way to create a better life for *our* children is to fight for others' children. We must center all the children in our vision of a better future. And when we let the love for all children lead, we have a shot at getting there. To that place of great possibility, inclusivity, integrity, prosperity. One nation. Under God. Indivisible.

The grandest cathedrals take a long time to build. The good news about ours is that it's still very much under construction. The dustups that happen in our society and culture are evident of the urgent and necessary work underway. A physical sign might read "Pardon Our Progress" to signal that change is often inconvenient and uncomfortable yet necessary.

Sadly, in recent years, demagogues have been threatening to burn our cathedral down. And they have the ear of the people who have lost faith in the democratic process. When people are desperate, they often look to dictators. When times are tough, tyrants emerge, promising to fix things as no one else can. But we must resist their flattery, the narcissistic assertion of the singularity of their own voices and the messianic dimensions of their own abilities. They are not only false but contrary to the democratic process. Fighting for and preserving our democracy is our most urgent call to action.

But we must also take the long view. Will we have the moral fortitude to build on the work done by the great but imperfect patriots who preceded us? Will we have the vision and courage to continue building, brick by brick, an America of the people, by the people, and for the people? Or will the desires of a greedy few continue to dominate our national discourse as they now do, distorting the wants and needs of the many and rendering the rest of us without voice or vote?

My hope is to engage all our American family—people of all faiths and stripes and political persuasions. My hope is that the teachings of Isaiah will strike a collective chord within each of us, one that quickens the pace of change and inspires us to envision a wide and robust version of the future like none we've ever before imagined. My hope is that this book helps to spark and lead that family conversation.

I sometimes wonder about that neighbor who lived right next to me in Atlanta years ago with the AR-15-style weapon and what might have happened if I'd slowed down a bit from my public work and ministry of building the beloved community and had taken the time to actually get to know my next-door neighbor and his family. I wonder if we might have shared a meal one day and maybe even traded thoughts and feelings about guns and gun violence. I wonder if such a meeting, such a basic human connection, might have even led us both to a renewed sense of possibility; a renewed sense of what we might create together as an American people. As a pastor, a senator, and a parent, I wrestle with the same challenges as everyone else. I didn't really know my neighbor, and he didn't know me. But I do know this: We are not alone. We are all striving for something more. And we are all yearning for what is crooked in our lives to be made straight.

Across the years, I have learned with Rabbi Abraham Joshua Heschel, the great theologian and activist who through his words and his work sought to push people out of complacency, to pray with my legs. I have learned to put into practice the West African proverb that says, "When you pray, move your feet." But I also pray with my lips. Each morning, like clockwork, I pray. This time allows me to tap into my wellspring of faith and memory and enables me to keep going. When faced with seemingly intractable forces of oppression and injustice trying to overwhelm us by "flooding the zone," I remind myself of the arc of faith's testimony, embodied in the story of the cross and the resurrection, of Good Friday and

Easter Sunday. Evil always goes too far and therefore contains within itself the seed of its own destruction. My job is to keep bearing witness to love and keep building for justice. I remind myself that these challenges and battles didn't start with me and won't end with me. There were people of moral courage who came long before me, and who've been engaged in the good fight for our entire history as an American people.

I remind myself, as I pray, of words from Lamentations, written during a dark, difficult time of personal mourning and national loss. "But this I call to mind, and therefore I have hope: the steadfast love of the Lord never ceases, His mercies never come to an end; they are new every morning; great is your faithfulness." Part of what the writer invokes in this passage, and what I invoke in this book, is the power of collective, sacred memory. By calling to mind the struggles of the people before us, who had no reason to believe that they could overcome but kept marching anyway, we're infused with the strength and the faith to keep moving, to keep fighting.

In that sense, the first three words of our Constitution were not just the opening words to a sentence but spelled the beginning of a new chapter in human history. Let us not forget that those three words are in themselves a creed: We, the people. We must never allow anyone, or any movement, or any politician's self-serving ambitions, to rob us of our creed. We, the people.

In this dark and difficult moment in American history, in these times of crises that boggle the mind, I still believe in "we the people."

I still have faith in America.

I still believe that we shall overcome.

ACKNOWLEDGMENTS

This book began as a sermon preached in churches and temples, on college campuses and in community gatherings across the length and breadth of our nation. I am grateful to the people of my own congregation, Ebenezer Baptist Church, for hearing and responding to the earliest iteration of what was yet another Sunday-morning sermon and for the many congregations who have given feedback to variations of what has become this book, a sermon in the public square. In the best of my own church tradition, the preachment presupposes a dynamic of call-and-response, and I am grateful for the communal and congregational conversation partners I have already had along the way. Kristal Brent Zook and Donna Byrd were quite helpful early on as I thought through the framing of this work. Gary Dorrien, Obery Hendricks, and Rodney Sadler provided helpful feedback.

Yet, no conversation partner has been more important than

Lisa Frazier, a steady and able interlocutor who along with my editor, Virginia Smith, and book agent, Will Lippincott, enabled me to keep writing even while attending to my many other responsibilities between Georgia and Washington, DC. The team at Penguin Random House, including Gail Brussel and Iris Chen, facilitated the finishing of this project at every turn.

As a pastor who serves in the Senate, I know that the organic flow of my project, as a voice of faith and conscience in the Congress, seeking to weave high ethical ideals into public policy, simply would not be possible without my incredible staff. My heartfelt thanks to Esther Harris, John Vaughn, Mark Libell, Elena Radding, Josh Delaney, Annie Wang, Meredith Lilly, Bee Nguyen, Quentin Fulks, Adam Magnus, Stuart Guillory, Nicole Marquez, Brandon Gilkes, and the many other staff members who have worked with me in the Senate and in the church, both present and past. These reflections on the moral meaning of America are rooted in remembrances of some of the "good trouble" we have been blessed to get into together across the years.

My friends and my family, especially my two young children, always ensure that I do not take myself too seriously even while doing serious work. For that, they deserve credit, all errors and omissions are mine. My highest gratitude and praise to God, glimpses of whose face I see daily in the faces of our collective humanity, the yearnings of the American people, and all those I am blessed and honored to serve.

NOTES

INTRODUCTION: AMERICA, THE GRAND CATHEDRAL

xxiv **Tellingly, this latter group:** Gregory A. Smith et al., "Decline of Christianity in the U.S. Has Slowed, May Have Leveled Off," Pew Research Center, February 26, 2025, pewresearch.org/religion/2025/02/26/decline-of-christianity-in-the-us-has-slowed-may-have-leveled-off.

CHAPTER 1: A SPARK OF THE DIVINE

3 **In the early afternoon:** U.S. Government Accountability Office, "Capitol Attack: Federal Agencies Identified Some Threats, but Did Not Fully Process and Share Information Prior to January 6, 2021," GAO-23-106625, February 2023, 1, gao.gov/assets/gao-23-106625.pdf.

6 **In a journal kept by:** Julie Miller, "'A Republic if You Can Keep It': Elizabeth Willing Powel, Benjamin Franklin, and the James McHenry

Journal," *Unfolding History: Manuscripts at the Library of Congress* (blog), January 6, 2022, blogs.loc.gov/manuscripts/2022/01/a-republic-if-you-can-keep-it-elizabeth-willing-powel-benjamin-franklin-and-the-james-mchenry-journal.

10 **In the five years after:** Shelby County, Alabama v. Holder, 570 U.S. 529 (2013), tile.loc.gov/storage-services/service/ll/usrep/usrep570/usrep570529/usrep570529.pdf.

11 **Justice Ruth Bader Ginsburg:** Shelby County, Alabama v. Holder.

12 **That's exactly what happened:** Jon Ward, "How a Criminal Investigation in Georgia Set an Ominous Tone for African-American Voters," *Yahoo! News*, August 6, 2019, yahoo.com/news/how-a-criminal-investigation-in-georgia-set-a-dark-tone-for-african-american-voters-090000532.html.

16 **A record number of Georgians:** Legal Defense Fund, "LDF's Lawsuit Challenging Georgia's Voter Suppression Law," *Our Thinking*, April 7, 2021, naacpldf.org/naacp-publications/ldf-blog/important-facts-about-ldfs-lawsuit-challenging-georgias-voter-suppression-bill.

17 **In 2022, just six right-wing activists:** Doug Bock Clark, "Close to 100,000 Voter Registrations Were Challenged in Georgia—Almost All by Just Six Right-Wing Activists," *ProPublica*, July 13, 2023, propublica.org/article/right-wing-activists-georgia-voter-challenges.

18 **According to analysis:** Hannah Klain et al., "Waiting to Vote: Racial Disparities in Election Day Experiences," Brennan Center for Justice at New York University, June 3, 2020, brennancenter.org/our-work/research-reports/waiting-vote.

CHAPTER 2: SQUEEZING OUT "THE LEAST OF THESE"

29 **In January 2010, the nation's:** Daniel I. Weiner, "*Citizens United* Explained," Brennan Center for Justice, December 12, 2019, updated January 29, 2025, brennancenter.org/our-work/research-reports/citizens-united-explained.

30 **"As a result, the American":** Jane Mayer, *Dark Money: The Hidden History of the Billionaires Behind the Rise of the Radical Right* (Vintage Books, 2017), 281.

32 **The founder of Citizens United:** Sean Cockerham, "The Man Behind Willie Horton Ads Has New Target: Hillary Clinton," *McClatchy DC*, July 14, 2007, mcclatchydc.com/news/politics-government/article24466504.html.

33 **In 1988, Brown served:** Center for Media and Democracy, "Floyd G. Brown," SourceWatch, last edited December 25, 2019, sourcewatch.org/index.php/Floyd_G._Brown.

34 **The district court ruled against:** Federal Election Commission, "Citizens United v. FEC," FEC *Record*, February 2010, fec.gov/legal-resources/court-cases/citizens-united-v-fec.

34 **"At bottom, the Court's opinion":** Citizens United v. FEC, 558 US 310 (2010), supreme.justia.com/cases/federal/us/558/310.

35 **He retired from business:** United States Senate, "Mark Hanna and the 1896 Election," n.d., senate.gov/artandhistory/history/minute/Hanna_1896Election.htm.

36 **During that campaign:** J. Michael Bitzer, "Tillman Act of 1907,"

Free Speech Center at Middle Tennessee State University, January 1, 2009, last updated July 2, 2024, firstamendment.mtsu.edu/article/tillman-act-of-1907.

36 **But the next year:** "The Campaign Fund Scandal," *New York Times*, September 17, 1905, 8, nytimes.com/1905/09/17/archives/the-campaign-fund-scandal.html.

37 **Even if adjusted for inflation:** Theodore Schleifer and Albert Sun, "How Much Did Trump, Harris and Biden Raise? A Stunning $4.7 Billion," *New York Times*, December 6, 2021, nytimes.com/2024/12/06/us/politics/trump-harris-campaign-fundraising.html.

40 **Leo was spurred:** Andy Kroll, Andrea Bernstein, and Ilva Marritz, "We Don't Talk About Leonard: The Man Behind the Right's Supreme Court Supermajority," *ProPublica*, October 11, 2023, propublica.org/article/we-dont-talk-about-leonard-leo-supreme-court-supermajority.

40 **Perhaps more than any:** Kroll, Bernstein, and Marritz, "We Don't Talk About Leonard."

40 **All six of the current:** "The Conservative Club That Came to Dominate the Supreme Court," *The Harvard Gazette*, March 4, 2021, news.harvard.edu/gazette/story/2021/03/in-audiobook-takeover-noah-feldman-lidia-jean-kott-explore-how-federalist-society-captured-supreme-court.

42 **According to the former:** Ann Ravel, "Departing the Federal Election Commission," *Medium*, February 19, 2017, medium.com/@AnnMRavel/departing-the-federal-election-commission-fee0ae9d63a1.

42 **In 2006, for example:** Weiner, "*Citizens United* Explained."

42 **But in the 2024 presidential:** Anna Massoglia, "Dark Money Hit a Record High of $1.9 Billion in 2024 Federal Races," Brennan Center for Justice, May 7, 2025, brennancenter.org/our-work/research-reports/dark-money-hit-record-high-19-billion-2024-federal-races.

42 **Elon Musk, then the richest:** Trisha Thadani, Clara Ence Morse, and Maeve Reston, "Elon Musk Donated $288 Million in 2024 Election, Final Tally Shows," *Washington Post*, January 31, 2025, washingtonpost.com/politics/2025/01/31/elon-musk-trump-donor-2024-election.

44 **In 2025, there were:** OpenSecrets, "Lobbying Data Summary," n.d., opensecrets.org/federal-lobbying.

CHAPTER 3: TWO THOUSAND VERSES

52 **around 37 million Americans:** Emily A. Shrider, "Poverty in the United States: 2023," U.S. Census Bureau, 2024, census.gov/library/publications/2024/demo/p60-283.html.

52 **Meanwhile, the number of billionaires:** Chuck Collins, "Updates: Billionaire Wealth, U.S. Job Losses and Pandemic Profiteers," Inequality.org, March 18, 2024, inequality.org/article/updates-billionaire/#:~:text=There%20are%20now%2015%20U.S.,combined%20wealth%20of%20$121.1%20billion.

52 **And in 2024:** Pallavi Rao, "A Visual Breakdown of Who Owns America's Wealth," *Visual Capitalist*, March 4, 2025, visualcapitalist.com/a-visual-breakdown-of-who-owns-americas-wealth.

52 **That same 1 percent:** "Wealth Inequality in the United States," Inequality.org, inequality.org/facts/wealth-inequality/#richest-americans.

54 **The great abolitionist:** Frederick Douglass, *Narrative of the Life of Frederick Douglass, an American Slave* (Anti-Slavery Office, 1849).

55 **"For of all":** Douglass, *Narrative of the Life of Frederick Douglass*, 78.

60 **But nearly fourteen million children:** U.S. Department of Agriculture, "Food Security in the U.S.," updated January 8, 2025.

66 **When I drafted the AIRWAYS legislation:** "Aircraft Pilots & Flight Engineers," DATA USA, 2023, datausa.io/profile/soc/aircraft-pilots-flight-engineers?ethnicity-gender=genderAllE&races-filter=genderraceR.

68 **"Right now, opportunity":** Raj Chetty, "I Have Studied Social Mobility for Years. Here's How Kamala Harris Can Build An 'Opportunity Economy,'" *New York Times*, September 20, 2024, https://www.nytimes.com/2024/09/20/opinion/kamala-harris-opportunity-economy.html.

72 **"the story of chosen scarcities":** Ezra Klein and Derek Thompson, *Abundance* (Simon & Schuster, 2025), 4, 8.

CHAPTER 4: SCAR ON THE SOUL OF AMERICA

78 **This nation makes up:** NAACP, "Criminal Justice Fact Sheet," n.d., naacp.org/resources/criminal-justice-fact-sheet.

78 **And a disproportionate share:** Wendy Sawyer and Peter Wagner, "Mass Incarceration: The Whole Pie 2025," Prison Policy Initiative, March 11, 2025, prisonpolicy.org/graphs/pie2025_race_bar.html.

85 **police department was more motivated:** U.S. Department of Justice Civil Rights Division, "Investigation of the Ferguson Police Department," March 4, 2015, justice.gov/sites/default/files/opa/press-releases/attachments/2015/03/04/ferguson_police_department_report.pdf.

86 **I can't help but think:** "Kalief Browder," Say Their Names, Stanford University Libraries, exhibits.stanford.edu/saytheirnames/feature/kalief-browder.

89 **While there has been:** This figure was derived by combining two key figures. Based on the Prison Policy Initiative's "Mass Incarceration: The Whole Pie 2025," nearly 2 million people are incarcerated in federal, state, local, and tribal jails and prison, and 41 percent of them, or 820,000 people, are black; 2.9 million people are on probation, plus 670,000 people on parole, totaling 3.6 million people under community control; 30 percent of those under community control, or 1.08 million, are black. Add that to the 820,000 black adults in prison, and you get a total of 1.9 million. Wendy Sawyer and Peter Wagner, "Mass Incarceration: The Whole Pie 2025," Prison Policy Initiative, March 11, 2025, prisonpolicy.org/reports/pie2025.html#tenthmyth.

96 **According to a report written:** Senator Cory A. Booker, "CARES Act: Home Confinement Three Years Later," June 2023, booker.senate.gov/imo/media/doc/cares_act_home_confinement_policy_brief1.pdf.

CHAPTER 5: GUNS EVERYWHERE

109 **In 2024, there were 503:** Gun Violence Archive, "Gun Violence Archive, 2024," August 29, 2025, gunviolencearchive.org/past-tolls.

109 **"We are caught in an inescapable":** Martin Luther King Jr., "Letter from a Birmingham Jail," April 16, 1963, available at African Studies Center, University of Pennsylvania, africa.upenn.edu/Articles_Gen/Letter_Birmingham.html.

110 **survivor Ashbey Beasley:** Senator Raphael Warnock, "Senator Reverend Warnock, Congressional Lawmakers and Advocates Lift Up Survivor Stories to Urge Congress Not to Turn Away from Recent Gun Violence Tragedies," press release, May 23, 2023, warnock.senate.gov/newsroom/press-releases/watch-senator-reverend-warnock-congressional-lawmakers-and-advocates-lift-up-survivor-stories-to-urge-congress-not-to-turn-away-from-recent-gun-violence-tragedie.

111 **In 2024, a total of 41,033:** Gun Violence Archive, "Gun Violence Archive, 2024."

112 **Across this nation, 17,927 people:** CDC National Center for Health Statistics, "Assault or Homicide," last reviewed January 17, 2025, cdc.gov/nchs/fastats/homicide.htm#:~:text=All%20homicides%20*%20Number%20of%20deaths:%2022%2C830.%20*%20Deaths%20per%20100%2C000%20population:%206.8.

112 **Young black men between the ages:** "The Disproportionate Impact of Gun Violence on Black Americans," Brady, bradyunited.org/resources/research/disproportionate-impact-gun-violence-black-americans.

112 **The grim truth:** Alexia Cooper and Erica L. Smith, "Homicide Trends in the United States, 1980–2008," U.S. Department of Justice, November 2011, bjs.ojp.gov/content/pub/pdf/htus8008.pdf.

114 **more guns than people:** Harmeet Kaur, "What Studies Reveal About Gun Ownership in the US," CNN, June 2, 2022, cnn.com/2022/06/02/us/gun-ownership-numbers-us-cec#:~:text=Only%20a%20few%20gun%20owners,purchases%20are%20at%20record%20highs.

118 **We are stunned by the fact:** Nirmita Panchal and Sasha Zitter, "The Impact of Gun Violence on Children and Adolescents," KFF, May 27, 2025, kff.org/mental-health/the-impact-of-gun-violence-on-children-and-adolescents.

118 **In 2023, after:** Kelly McEvers, host, "Supermajority: The Covenant Moms," *Embedded*, National Public Radio, June 18, 2024, npr.org/transcripts/1200150197.

120 **He told a local newspaper:** Abby Livingston, "Texas Congressman Tony Gonzales, Who Represents Uvalde, Breaks with House Republicans to Vote for Gun Bill," *Texas Tribune*, June 24, 2022, texastribune.org/2022/06/24/bipartisan-gun-legislation-tony-gonzales.

CHAPTER 6: HUMBLE OURSELVES, HEAL THE LAND

127 **All that death and destruction:** Richard D. Knabb, Jamie R. Rhome, and Daniel P. Brown, "Tropical Cyclone Report: Hurricane Katrina,"

National Hurricane Center, January 4, 2023, nhc.noaa.gov/data/tcr/AL122005_Katrina.pdf.

128 **From its first successful:** Jason P. Theriot, "Oil and Gas Industry in Louisiana," *64 Parishes*, February 25, 2021, 64parishes.org/entry/oil-and-gas-industry-in-louisiana#:~:text=Louisiana's%20oil%20and%20gas%20industry,the%20way%20for%20the%20state.

128 **By the 1960s:** Tom Sanzillo, Suzanne Mattei, and Abhishek Sinha, "The Declining Significance of the Petrochemical Industry in Louisiana," Institute for Energy Economics and Financial Analysis, October 28, 2024, ieefa.org/resources/declining-significance-petrochemical-industry-louisiana.

129 **"When I initially arrived":** *Hurricane Katrina: Race Against Time*, directed by Traci A. Curry (National Geographic, 2025).

131 **The same fossil fuel and petrochemical:** Public Health on Call, "Louisiana's 'Cancer Alley' Is More Deadly Than Previously Imagined," Johns Hopkins Bloomberg School of Health, August 4, 2025, publichealth.jhu.edu/2025/the-shocking-hazards-of-louisianas-cancer-alley.

131 **The EPA even urged:** Amanda Watts, Andi Babineau, and Elizabeth Wolfe, "EPA Recommends Louisiana State Agencies Consider Relocating Elementary School Students over Toxic Chemical Exposure," CNN, October 26, 2022, cnn.com/2022/10/26/us/louisiana-laplace-school-chloroprene-chemical-exposure-reaj.

132 **In March 2021:** United Nations Human Rights Office of the High Commission, "USA: Environmental Racism in 'Cancer Alley' Must End—Experts," press release, March 2, 2021, ohchr.org/en/press

-releases/2021/03/usa-environmental-racism-cancer-alley-must-end -experts?LangID=E&NewsID=26824.

133 **But in 2023:** Jack Brook, "Lawsuit Alleging Environmental Racism in Louisiana Parish Allowed to Proceed, Federal Court Says," Associated Press, April 9, 2025, apnews.com/article/louisiana-st-james-parish -environmental-racism-cancer-alley-59c804bf7a1eda5e39d8f59225 13f6f6.

134 **Experts tell us that:** United Nations Climate Action, "Causes and Effects of Climate Change," un.org/en/climatechange/science/causes -effects-climate-change.

134 **The average surface temperature:** National Aeronautics and Space Administration, "Evidence," n.d., science.nasa.gov/climate-change /evidence.

135 **The agency's satellites show:** National Aeronautics and Space Administration, "Evidence."

139 **He stirred up good trouble:** Jessica Dortch, "'Transfigured Moments' with Vernon Johns," *Afro News*, January 15, 2021, afro.com /transfigured-moments-with-vernon-johns.

147 **Within a decade, this planet:** United Nations Department of Economic and Social Affairs, "World Population Projected to Reach 9.8 Billion in 2050, and 11.2 Billion in 2100," revised 2017, un.org /en/desa/world-population-projected-reach-98-billion-2050-and-112 -billion-2100.

INDEX